Richard Harding Davis

Stories for boys

Richard Harding Davis

Stories for boys

ISBN/EAN: 9783743304871

Manufactured in Europe, USA, Canada, Australia, Japa

Cover: Foto ©ninafisch / pixelio.de

Manufactured and distributed by brebook publishing software (www.brebook.com)

Richard Harding Davis

Stories for boys

"I never saw a King," Gordon remarked, "and I'm sure I never expected to see one sitting on a log in the rain."

STORIES FOR BOYS

BY

RICHARD HARDING DAVIS

ILLUSTRATED

NEW YORK
CHARLES SCRIBNER'S SONS
1896

COPYRIGHT, 1891, BY

CHARLES SCRIBNER'S SONS.

THIS BOOK OF BOYS' STORIES IS DEDICATED
TO MY BROTHER

C. BELMONT DAVIS

WHO WAS A BOY ABOUT THE SAME TIME I WAS

CONTENTS.

	PAGE
THE REPORTER WHO MADE HIMSELF KING	1
MIDSUMMER PIRATES	88
RICHARD CARR'S BABY	117
THE GREAT TRI-CLUB TENNIS TOURNAMENT	130
THE JUMP AT COREY'S SLIP	166
THE VAN BIBBER BASEBALL CLUB	177
THE STORY OF A JOCKEY	184

LIST OF ILLUSTRATIONS.

"I never saw a King" Gordon remarked, "and I'm sure I never expected to see one sitting on a log in the rain," *Frontispiece*

PAGE

"About time to begin on the goats!" . . 44

To the North towered three magnificent hulls of the White Squadron, . . . 86

"Which do I think will win?" said the veteran boat-builder of Manasquan, . 96

As the two Prescotts scrambled up on the gunwale of their boat, the defeated crew saluted them with cheers, . . . 112

He took a large roll of bills from his pocket and counted them, ... 198

THE REPORTER WHO MADE HIMSELF KING.

The Old Time Journalist will tell you the best reporter is the one who works his way up. He will hold that the only way to start is as a printer's devil, or as an office boy, to learn in time to set type, to graduate from a compositor into a stenographer, and as a stenographer take down speeches at public meetings, and so finally grow into a real reporter, with a fire badge on your left suspender, and a speaking acquaintance with all the greatest men in the city, not even excepting Police Captains.

That is the old time journalist's idea of it. That is the way he was trained, and that is why he is reporting still. If you train up a youth in this way, he will go into reporting with too full a knowledge of the newspaper business, with no illusions concerning it, and with no ignorant enthusiasms, but with a keen and justifiable impression that he is

not paid enough for what he does. And he
will only do what he is paid to do. Now,
you cannot pay a good reporter for what he
does, because he does not work for pay. He
works for his paper. He gives his time, his
health, his brains, his sleeping hours, and his
eating hours, and life sometimes, to get news
for it. He thinks the sun rises only that men
may have light by which to read it. But if
he has been in a newspaper office from his
youth up, he finds out before he becomes a
reporter that this is not so, and loses his real
value. He should come right out of the
University where he has been doing "campus
notes" for the college weekly, and be pitch-
forked out into city work without knowing
whether the Battery is at Harlem or Hunter's
Point, and with the idea that he is a Moulder
of Public Opinion and that the Power of the
Press is greater than the Power of Money,
and that the few lines he writes are of more
value in the Editor's eyes than the column
of advertising on the last page, which they
are not. After three years — it is sometimes
longer, sometimes not so long — he finds out
that he has given his nerves and his youth
and his enthusiasm in exchange for a general

fund of miscellaneous knowledge, the opportunity of personal encounter with all the greatest and most remarkable men and events that have risen in those three years, and a great readiness of resource, and patience. He will find that he has crowded the experiences of the lifetime of the ordinary young business man, doctor, or lawyer, or man about town, into three short years; that he has learnt to think and to act quickly, to be patient and unmoved when every one else has lost his head, actually or figuratively speaking; to write as fast as another man can talk, and to be able to talk with authority on matters of which other men do not venture even to think until they have read what he has written with a copy-boy at his elbow on the night previous.

It is necessary for you to know this, that you may understand what manner of young man young Albert Gordon was.

Young Gordon had been a reporter just three years. He had left Yale when his last living relative died, and taken the morning train for New York, where they had promised him reportorial work on one of the innumerable Greatest New York Dailies. He arrived

at the office at noon, and was sent back over
the same road on which he had just come, to
Spuyten Duyvil, where a train had been
wrecked and about everybody of consequence
to suburban New York killed. One of the
old reporters hurried him to the office again
with his "copy," and after he had delivered
that, he was sent to the Tombs to talk French
to a man in Murderer's Row, who could not
talk anything else, but who had shown some
international skill in the use of a jimmy.
And at eight, he covered a flower show in
Madison Square Garden; and at eleven was
sent over the Brooklyn Bridge in a cab to
watch a fire and make guesses at the insurance.

He went to bed at one, and dreamt of shattered locomotives, human beings lying still with blankets over them, rows of cells, and banks of beautiful flowers nodding their heads to the tunes of the brass band in the gallery. He decided when he awoke the next morning that he had entered upon a picturesque and exciting career, and as one day followed another, he became more and more convinced of it, and more and more devoted to it. He was eighteen then, and he was now twenty-one, and in that time had become a great reporter, and had been to Presidential conventions in Chicago, revolutions in Hayti, Indian outbreaks on the Plains, and midnight meetings of moonlighters in Tennessee, and had seen what work earthquakes, floods, fire, and fever could do in great cities, and had contradicted the President, and borrowed matches from burglars. And now he thought he would like to rest and breathe a bit, and not to work again unless as a war correspondent or as a novelist. He had always had enough money of his own to keep him alive, and so he was in consequence independent of what the paper gave him. The only obstacle to his becoming a great war correspondent lay in the fact that there was no war, and a war correspondent without a war is about as absurd an individual as a general without an army. He read the papers every morning on the elevated trains for war clouds; but though there were many war clouds, they always drifted apart, and peace smiled again. This was very disappointing to young Gordon, and he was more and more keenly discouraged.

And then as war work was out of the question, he decided to write his novel. It was to be a novel of New York life, and he

wanted a quiet place in which to work on it.
He was already making inquiries among the
suburban residents of his acquaintance for
just such a quiet spot, when he received an
offer to go to the Island of Opeki in the
South Pacific Ocean, as secretary to the
American consul to that place. The gentleman who had been appointed by the President
to act as consul at Opeki, was Captain
Leonard T. Travis, a veteran of the Civil
War, who had contracted a severe attack of
rheumatism while camping out at night in the
dew, and who on account of this souvenir of
his efforts to save the Union had allowed the
Union he had saved to support him in one
office or another ever since. He had met
young Gordon at a dinner, and had had the
presumption to ask him to serve as his secretary, and Gordon, much to his surprise, had
accepted his offer. The idea of a quiet life
in the tropics with new and beautiful sur-
roundings, and with nothing to do and plenty
of time in which to do it, and to write his
novel besides, seemed to Albert to be just
what he wanted; and though he did not know
or care much for his superior officer, he agreed
to go with him promptly, and proceeded to bid

good by to his friends and to make his preparations. Captain Travis was so delighted with getting such a clever young gentleman for his secretary, that he referred to him to his friends as "my attaché of legation"; nor did he lessen that gentleman's dignity by telling any one that the attaché's salary was to be $500 a year. His own salary was only $1500; and though his brother-in-law, Senator Rainsford, tried his best to get it raised, he was unsuccessful. The consulship to Opeki was instituted early in the '50's, to get rid of and reward a third or fourth cousin of the President's, whose services during the campaign were important, but whose after-presence was embarrassing. He had been created consul to Opeki as being more distant and unaccessible than any other known spot, and had lived and died there; and so little was known of the island, and so difficult was communication with it, that no one knew he was dead, until Captain Travis, in his hungry haste for office, had uprooted the sad fact. Captain Travis, as well as Albert, had a secondary reason for wishing to visit Opeki. His physician had told him to go to some warm climate for his rheumatism, and in accepting the consulship his object was rather to follow out his doctor's orders at his country's expense, than to serve his country at the expense of his rheumatism.

Albert could learn but very little of Opeki; nothing, indeed, but that it was situated about one hundred miles from the Island of Octavia, which island, in turn, was simply described as a coaling-station three hundred miles from the coast of California. Steamers from San Francisco to Yokohama stopped every third week at Octavia, and that was all either Captain Travis or his secretary could learn of their new home. This was so very little, that Albert stipulated to stay only as long as he liked it, and to return to the States within a few months if he found such a change of plan desirable.

As he was going to what was an almost undiscovered country, he thought it would be a good plan to furnish himself with a supply of articles with which to trade with the native Opekians, and for this purpose he purchased a large quantity of brass rods, because he had read that Stanley did so, and added to these, brass curtain chains and about two hundred leaden medals similar to those sold by street pedlers during the Constitutional

Centennial celebration in New York City, and which were cheap. He also collected even more beautiful but less expensive decorations for Christmas trees, at a wholesale house on Park Row. These he hoped to exchange for furs or feathers or weapons, or for whatever other curious and valuable trophies the Island of Opeki boasted. He already pictured his room on his return hung fantastically with crossed spears and boomerangs, feather head-dresses, and ugly idols. His friends told him he was doing a very foolish thing, and argued that once out of the newspaper world, it would be hard to regain his place in it. But he thought the novel he would write while lost to the world at Opeki would serve to make up for his temporary absence from it, and he expressly and impressively stipulated that the editor should wire him if there was a war.

Captain Travis and his secretary crossed the continent without adventure, and took passage from San Francisco on the first steamer that touched Octavia. They reached that island in three days, and learned with some concern that there was no regular communication with Opeki, and that it would be necessary to charter a sail-boat for the trip. Two fishermen agreed to take them and their trunks, and to get them to their destination within sixteen hours if the wind held good. It was a most unpleasant sail. The rain fell with calm, relentless persistence from what was apparently a clear sky; the wind tossed the waves as high as the mast and made Captain Travis ill. There was no deck to the big boat, and they were forced to huddle up under pieces of canvas, and talked but little. Captain Travis complained of frequent twinges of rheumatism, and gazed forlornly over the gunwale at the empty waste of water.

"If I've got to serve a term of imprisonment on a rock in the middle of the ocean for four years," he said, "I might just as well have done something first, to deserve it. This is a pretty way to treat a man who bled for his country. This is gratitude, this is." Albert pulled heavily on his pipe, and wiped the rain and spray from his face and smiled.

"Oh, it won't be so bad when we get there," he said; "they say these Southern people are always hospitable, and the whites will be glad to see any one from the States."

"There will be a round of diplomatic dinners," said the consul, with an attempt at cheerfulness. "I have brought two uniforms to wear at them."

It was seven o'clock in the evening when the rain ceased, and one of the black, half-naked fishermen nodded and pointed at a little low line on the horizon.

"Opeki," he said. The line grew in length until it proved to be an island with great mountains rising to the clouds, and as they drew nearer and nearer, showed a level coast running back to the foot of the mountains and covered with a forest of palms. They next made out a village of thatched huts around a grassy square, and at some distance from the village a wooden structure with a tin roof.

"I wonder where the town is," asked the consul, with a nervous glance at the fishermen. One of them told him that what he saw was the town.

"That?" gasped the consul; "is that where all the people on the island live?" The fisherman nodded; but the other added that there were other natives up in the mountains, but that they were bad men who fought and ate each other. The consul and his attaché of legation gazed at the mountains with unspoken misgivings. They were quite near now, and could see an immense crowd of men and women, all of them black, and clad but in the simplest garments, waiting to receive them. They seemed greatly excited and ran in and out of the huts, and up and down the beach, as wildly as so many black ants. But in the front of the group they distinguished three men who they could see were white, though they were clothed like the others, simply in a shirt and a short pair of trousers. Two of these three suddenly sprang away on a run and disappeared among the palm trees; but the third one, who had recognized the American flag in the halyards, threw his straw hat in the water and began turning handsprings over the sand.

"That young gentleman, at least," said Albert, gravely, "seems pleased to see us."

A dozen of the natives sprang into the water and came wading and swimming towards them, and grinning and shouting and swinging their arms.

"I don't think it's quite safe, do you?" said the consul, looking out wildly to the open sea. "You see, they don't know who I am."

A great black giant threw one arm over the gunwale and shouted something that sounded as if it were spelt Owah, Owah, as the boat carried him through the surf.

"How do you do?" said Gordon, doubtfully. The boat shook the giant off under the wave and beached itself so suddenly that the American consul was thrown forward to his knees. Gordon did not wait to pick him up, but jumped out and shook hands with the young man who had turned handsprings, while the natives gathered about them in a circle and chatted and laughed in delighted excitement.

"I'm awful glad to see you," said the young man, eagerly. "My name's Stedman. I'm from New Haven, Connecticut. Where are you from?"

"New York," said Albert. "This," he added, pointing solemnly to Captain Travis, who was still on his knees in the boat, "is the American consul to Opeki." The American consul to Opeki gave a wild look at Mr. Stedman of New Haven and at the natives.

"See here, young man," he gasped, "is this all there is of Opeki?"

"The American consul?" said young Stedman, with a gasp of amazement, and looking from Albert to Captain Travis. "Why, I never supposed they would send another here; the last one died about fifteen years ago, and there hasn't been one since. I've been living in the consul's office with the Bradleys, but I'll move out, of course. I'm sure I'm awfully glad to see you It'll make it more pleasant for me."

"Yes," said Captain Travis, bitterly, as he lifted his rheumatic leg over the boat; "that's why we came."

Mr. Stedman did not notice this He was too much pleased to be anything but hospitable. "You are soaking wet, aren't you?" he said; "and hungry, I guess. You come right over to the consul's office and get on some other things."

He turned to the natives and gave some rapid orders in their language, and some of them jumped into the boat at this, and began lifting out the trunks, and others ran off towards a large, stout old native, who was sitting gravely on a log, smoking, with the rain beating unnoticed on his gray hair.

"They've gone to tell the King," said Stedman; "but you both better get something to eat first, and then I'll be happy to present you properly."

"The King," said Captain Travis, with some awe; "is there a king?"

"I never saw a king," Gordon remarked, "and I'm sure I never expected to see one sitting on a log in the rain."

"He's a very good King," said Stedman, confidentially; "and though you mightn't think it to look at him, he's a terrible stickler for etiquette and form. After supper he'll give you an audience; and if you have any tobacco, you had better give him some as a present, and you'd better say it's from the President: he doesn't like to take presents from common people, he's so proud. The only reason he borrows mine is because he thinks I'm the President's son."

"What makes him think that?" demanded the consul, with some shortness. Young Mr. Stedman looked nervously at the consul and at Albert, and said that he guessed some one must have told him. The consul's office was divided into four rooms with an open court in the middle, filled with palms, and watered somewhat unnecessarily by a fountain.

"I made that," said Stedman, in a modest off-hand way. "I made it out of hollow bamboo reeds connected with a spring. And now I'm making one for the King. He saw this and had a lot of bamboo sticks put up all over the town, without any underground connections, and couldn't make out why the water wouldn't spurt out of them. And because mine spurts, he thinks I'm a magician."

"I suppose," grumbled the consul, "some one told him that, too."

"I suppose so," said Mr. Stedman, uneasily.

There was a veranda around the consul's office, and inside, the walls were hung with skins, and pictures from illustrated papers, and there was a good deal of bamboo furniture, and four broad, cool-looking beds. The place was as clean as a kitchen. "I made the furniture," said Stedman, "and the Bradleys keep the place in order."

"Who are the Bradleys?" asked Albert.

"The Bradleys are those two men you saw with me," said Stedman; "they deserted from a British man-of-war that stopped here for coal, and they act as my servants. One is Bradley, Sr., and the other, Bradley, Jr."

"Then vessels do stop here, occasionally?" the consul said, with a pleased smile.

"Well, not often," said Stedman. "Not so very often; about once a year. The *Nelson* thought this was Octavia, and put off again as soon as she found out her mistake, and the Bradleys took to the bush, and the boat's crew couldn't find them. When they saw your flag, they thought you might mean to send them back, so they ran off to hide again: they'll be back, though, when they get hungry."

The supper young Stedman spread for his guests, as he still treated them, was very refreshing and very good. There was cold fish and pigeon pie, and a hot omelet filled with mushrooms and olives and tomatoes and onions all sliced up together, and strong black coffee. After supper, Stedman went off to see the King and came back in a little while to say that his Majesty would give them an audience the next day after breakfast. "It is too dark now," Stedman explained; "and it's raining so that they can't make the street lamps burn. Did you happen to notice our lamps? I invented them; but they don't work very well, yet. I've got the right idea, though, and I'll soon have the town illuminated all over, whether it rains or not."

The consul had been very silent and indifferent, during supper, to all around him. Now he looked up with some show of interest.

"How much longer is it going to rain, do you think?" he asked.

"Oh, I don't know," said Stedman, critically. "Not more than two months, I should say." The consul rubbed his rheumatic leg and sighed, but said nothing.

The Bradleys turned up about ten o'clock, and came in very sheepishly, pulling at their forelocks and scraping with their left foot. The consul had gone off to pay the boatmen who had brought them, and Albert in his absence assured the sailors that there was not the least danger of their being sent away. Then he turned into one of the beds, and Stedman took one in another room, leaving the room he had occupied heretofore, for the consul. As he was saying good night, Albert suggested that he had not yet told them how he came to be on a deserted island; but Stedman only laughed and said that that was a long story, and that he would tell him all about it in the morning. So Albert went off to bed without waiting for the consul to return, and fell asleep, wondering at the strangeness of his new life, and assuring himself that if the rain only kept up, he would have his novel finished in a month.

The sun was shining brightly when he awoke, and the palm trees outside were nodding gracefully in a warm breeze. From the court came the odor of strange flowers, and from the window he could see the ocean brilliantly blue, and with the sun coloring the spray that beat against the coral reefs on the shore.

"Well, the consul can't complain of this," he said, with a laugh of satisfaction; and pulling on a bath-robe, he stepped into the next room to awaken Captain Travis. But the room was quite empty, and the bed undisturbed. The consul's trunk remained just where it had been placed near the door, and on it lay a large sheet of foolscap, with writing on it, and addressed at the top to

Albert Gordon. The handwriting was the
consul's. Albert picked it up and read it
with much anxiety. It began abruptly: —

"The fishermen who brought us to this
forsaken spot tell me that it rains here six
months in the year, and that this is the first
month. I came here to serve my country,
for which I fought and bled, but I did not
come here to die of rheumatism and pneumo-
nia. I can serve my country better by stay-
ing alive; and whether it rains or not, I don't
like it. I have been grossly deceived, and I
am going back. Indeed, by the time you get
this, I will be on my return trip, as I intend
leaving with the men who brought us here as
soon as they can get the sail up. My cousin,
Senator Rainsford, can fix it all right with
the President, and can have me recalled in
proper form after I get back. But of course
it would not do for me to leave my post with
no one to take my place, and no one could be
more ably fitted to do so than yourself; so I
feel no compunctions at leaving you behind.
I hereby, therefore, accordingly appoint you
my substitute with full power to act, to
collect all fees, sign all papers, and attend

to all matters pertaining to your office as American consul, and I trust you will worthily uphold the name of that country and government which it has always been my pleasure and duty to serve.

"Your sincere friend and superior officer,
"LEONARD T. TRAVIS.

"P.S. I did not care to disturb you by moving my trunk, so I left it, and you can make what use you please of whatever it contains, as I shall not want tropical garments where I am going. What you will need most, I think, is a waterproof and umbrella.

"P.S. Look out for that young man Stedman. He is too inventive. I hope you will like your high office; but as for me, I am satisfied with little old New York. Opeki is just a bit too far from civilization to suit me."

Albert held the letter before him and read it over again before he moved. Then he jumped to the window. The boat was gone, and there was not a sign of it on the horizon.

"The miserable old hypocrite!" he cried, half angry and half laughing. "If he thinks I am going to stay here alone he is very greatly mistaken. And yet, why not?" he asked. He stopped soliloquizing and looked around him, thinking rapidly. As he stood there, Stedman came in from the other room, fresh and smiling from his morning's bath.

"Good morning," he said, "where's the consul?"

"The consul," said Albert, gravely, "is before you. In me you see the American consul to Opeki."

"Captain Travis," Albert explained, "has returned to the United States. I suppose he feels that he can best serve his country by remaining on the spot. In case of another war, now, for instance, he would be there to save it again."

"And what are you going to do?" asked Stedman, anxiously. "You will not run away too, will you?"

Albert said that he intended to remain where he was and perform his consular duties, to appoint him his secretary of legation, and to elevate the United States in the opinion of the Opekians above all other nations.

"They may not think much of the United States in Russia," he said; "but we are going to teach Opeki that America is first on the map, and there is no second."

"I'm sure it's very good of you to make me your secretary," said Stedman, with some pride. "I hope I won't make any mistakes. What are the duties of a consul's secretary?"

"That," said Albert, "I do not know. But you are rather good at inventing, so you can invent a few. That should be your first duty, and you should attend to it at once. I will have trouble enough finding work for myself. Your salary is $500 a year; and now," he continued, briskly, "we want to prepare for this reception. We can tell the King that Travis was just a guard of honor for the trip, and that I have sent him back to tell the President of my safe arrival. That will keep the President from getting anxious. There is nothing," continued Albert, "like a uniform to impress people who live in the tropics, and Travis, it so happens, has two in his trunk. He intended to wear them on State occasions, and as I inherit the trunk and all that is in it, I intend to wear one of the uniforms, and you can have the other. But I have first choice, because I am consul."

Captain Travis's diplomatic outfit consisted of one full dress and one undress United

States uniform. Albert put on the dress coat over a pair of white flannel trousers, and looked remarkably brave and handsome. Stedman, who was only eighteen and quite thin, did not appear so well, until Albert suggested his padding out his chest and shoulders with towels. This made him rather warm, but helped his general appearance.

"The two Bradleys must dress up too," said Albert. "I think they ought to act as a guard of honor, don't you? The only things I have are blazers and jerseys; but it doesn't much matter what they wear, as long as they dress alike."

He accordingly called in the two Bradleys, and gave them each a pair of the captain's rejected white duck trousers, and a blue jersey apiece, with a big white Y on it.

"The students of Yale gave me that," he said to the younger Bradley, "in which to play football, and a great man gave me the other. His name is Walter Camp; and if you rip or soil that jersey, I'll send you back to England in irons; so be careful."

Stedman gazed at his companions in their different costumes, doubtfully. "It reminds me," he said, "of private theatricals. Of the time our church choir played 'Pinafore.'"

"Yes," assented Albert; "but I don't think we look quite gay enough. I tell you what we need, — medals. You never saw a diplomat without a lot of decorations and medals."

"Well, I can fix that," Stedman said. "I've got a bag full. I used to be the fastest bicycle-rider in Connecticut, and I've got all my prizes with me."

Albert said doubtfully that that wasn't exactly the sort of medal he meant.

"Perhaps not," returned Stedman, as he began fumbling in his trunk; "but the King won't know the difference. He couldn't tell a cross of the Legion of Honor from a medal for the tug of war."

So the bicycle medals, of which Stedman seemed to have an innumerable quantity, were strung in profusion over Albert's uniform, and in a lesser quantity over Stedman's; while a handful of leaden ones, those sold on the streets for the Constitutional Centennial, with which Albert had provided himself, were wrapped up in a red silk handkerchief for presentation to the King: with them Albert placed a number of brass rods and brass chains, much to Stedman's delighted approval.

"That is a very good idea," he said. "Democratic simplicity is the right thing at home, of course; but when you go abroad and mix with crowned heads, you want to show them that you know what's what."

"Well," said Albert, gravely, "I sincerely hope this crowned head don't know what's what. If he reads 'Connecticut Agricultural State Fair. One mile bicycle race. First Prize,' on this badge, when we are trying to make him believe it's a war medal, it may hurt his feelings."

Bradley, Jr., went ahead to announce the approach of the American embassy, which he did with so much manner that the King deferred the audience a half-hour, in order that he might better prepare to receive his visitors. When the audience did take place, it attracted the entire population to the green spot in front of the King's palace, and their delight and excitement over the appearance of the visitors was sincere and hearty. The King was too polite to appear much surprised, but he showed his delight over his presents as simply and openly as a child. Thrice he insisted on embracing Albert, and kissing him three times on the forehead, which, Stedman assured him in a side whisper, was a great honor; an honor which was not extended to the secretary, although he was given a necklace of animals' claws instead, with which he was better satisfied.

After this reception, the embassy marched back to the consul's office, surrounded by an immense number of the natives, some of whom ran ahead and looked back at them, and crowded so close on them that the two Bradleys had to poke at the nearest ones with their guns. The crowd remained outside the office even after the procession of four had disappeared, and cheered. This suggested to Gordon that this would be a good time to make a speech, which he accordingly did, Stedman translating it, sentence by sentence. At the conclusion of this effort, Albert distributed a number of brass rings among the married men present, which they placed on whichever finger fitted best, and departed delighted.

Albert had wished to give the rings to the married women, but Stedman pointed out to him that it would be much cheaper to give them to the married men; for while one woman could only have one husband, one man could have at least six wives.

"And now, Stedman," said Albert, after the mob had gone, "tell me what you are doing on this island."

"It's a very simple story," Stedman said. "I am the representative, or agent, or operator, for the Yokohama Cable Company. The Yokohama Cable Company is a company started in San Francisco, for the purpose of laying a cable to Yokohama. It is a stock company; and though it started out very well, the stock has fallen very low. Between ourselves, it is not worth over three or four cents. When the officers of the company found out that no one would buy their stock, and that no one believed in them or their scheme, they laid a cable to Octavia, and extended it on to this island. Then they said they had run out of ready money, and would wait until they got more before laying their cable any further. I do not think they ever will lay it any further, but that is none of my business. My business is to answer cable messages from San Francisco, so that the people who visit the home office can see at least a part of the cable is working. That sometimes impresses them, and they buy stock. There is another chap over in Octavia, who relays all my messages and all my replies to those messages that come to me through him from San Francisco. They never send a message unless they have brought some one to the office whom they want to impress, and who, they think, has money to invest in the Y. C. C. stock, and so we never go near the wire, except at three o'clock every afternoon. And then generally only to say 'How are you?' or 'It's raining,' or something like that. I've been saying 'It's raining' now for the last three months, but to-day I will say that the new consul has arrived. That will be a pleasant surprise for the chap in Octavia, for he must be tired hearing about the weather. He generally answers 'Here too,' or 'So you said,' or something like that. I don't know what he says to the home office. He's brighter than I am, and that's why they put him between the two ends. He can see that the messages are transmitted more fully and more correctly, in a way to please possible subscribers."

"Sort of copy editor," suggested Albert.

"Yes, something of that sort, I fancy," said Stedman.

They walked down to the little shed on the shore, where the Y. C. C. office was placed, at three that day, and Albert watched Stedman send off his message with much interest. The "chap at Octavia," on being informed that the American consul had arrived at Opeki, inquired somewhat disrespectfully, "Is it a life sentence?"

"What does he mean by that?" asked Albert.

"I suppose," said his secretary, doubtfully, "that he thinks it a sort of a punishment to be sent to Opeki. I hope you don't grow to think so."

"Opeki is all very well," said Gordon, "or it will be when we get things going our way."

As they walked back to the office, Albert noticed a brass cannon, perched on a rock at the entrance to the harbor. This had been put there by the last consul, but had not been fired for many years. Albert immediately ordered the two Bradleys to get it in order, and to rig up a flag-pole beside it, for one of his American flags, which they were to salute every night when they lowered it at sundown.

"And when we are not using it," he said, "the King can borrow it to celebrate with, if he doesn't impose on us too often. The royal salute ought to be twenty-one guns, I think; but that would use up too much powder, so he will have to content himself with two."

"Did you notice," asked Stedman that night, as they sat on the veranda of the consul's house, in the moonlight, "how the people bowed to us as we passed?"

"Yes," Albert said he had noticed it. "Why?"

"Well, they never saluted me," replied Stedman. "That sign of respect is due to the show we made at the reception."

"It is due to us, in any event," said the consul, severely. "I tell you, my secretary, that we, as the representatives of the United States government, must be properly honored on this island. We must become a power. And we must do so without getting into trouble with the King. We must make them honor him, too, and then as we push him up, we will push ourselves up at the same time."

"They don't think much of consuls in Opeki," said Stedman, doubtfully. "You see the last one was a pretty poor sort. He brought the office into disrepute, and it wasn't really until I came and told them what a fine country the United States was, that they had any opinion of it at all. Now we must change all that."

"That is just what we will do," said Albert. "We will transform Opeki into a powerful and beautiful city. We will make these people work. They must put up a palace for the King, and lay out streets, and build wharves, and drain the town properly, and light it. I haven't seen this patent lighting apparatus of yours, but you had better get to work at it at once, and I'll persuade the King to appoint you commissioner of highways and gas, with authority to make his people toil. And I," he cried, in free enthusiasm, "will organize a navy and a standing army. Only," he added, with a relapse of interest, "there isn't anybody to fight."

"There isn't?" said Stedman, grimly, with a scornful smile. "You just go hunt up old Messenwah and the Hillmen with your standing army once, and you'll get all the fighting you want."

"The Hillmen?" said Albert.

"The Hillmen are the natives that live up there in the hills," Stedman said, nodding his head towards the three high mountains at the other end of the island, that stood out blackly against the purple, moonlit sky. "There are nearly as many of them as there are Opekians, and they hunt and fight for a living and for the pleasure of it. They have an old rascal named Messenwah for a king, and they come down here about once every three months, and tear things up." Albert sprang to his feet.

"Oh, they do, do they?" he said, staring up at the mountain tops. "They come down here and tear up things, do they? Well, I think we'll stop that, I think we'll stop that! I don't care how many there are. I'll get the two Bradleys to tell me all they know about the drilling, to-morrow morning, and we'll drill these Opekians, and have sham battles, and attacks, and repulses, until I make a lot of wild, howling Zulus out of them. And when the Hillmen come down to pay their quarterly visit, they'll go back again on a run. At least some of them will," he added ferociously. "Some of them will stay right here."

"Dear me, dear me!" said Stedman, with awe; "you are a born fighter, aren't you?"

"Well, you wait and see," said Gordon; "may be I am. I haven't studied tactics of war and the history of battles, so that I might be a great war correspondent, without learning something. And there is only one king on this island, and that is old Ollypybus himself. And I'll go over and have a talk with him about it to-morrow."

Young Stedman walked up and down the length of the veranda, in and out of the moonlight, with his hands in his pockets, and his head on his chest. "You have me all stirred up, Gordon," he said; "you seem so confident and bold, and you're not so much older than I am, either."

"My training has been different; that's all," said the reporter.

"Yes," Stedman said bitterly; "I have been sitting in an office ever since I left school, sending news over a wire or a cable, and you have been out in the world, gathering it."

"And now," said Gordon, smiling, and putting his arm around the other boy's shoulders, "we are going to make news ourselves."

"There is one thing I want to say to you before you turn in," said Stedman. "Before you suggest all these improvements on Ollypybus, you must remember that he has ruled absolutely here for twenty years, and that he does not think much of consuls. He has only seen your predecessor and yourself. He likes you because you appeared with such dignity, and because of the presents; but if I were you, I wouldn't suggest these improvements as coming from yourself."

"I don't understand," said Gordon; "who could they come from?"

"Well," said Stedman, "if you will allow me to advise, — and you see I know these people pretty well, — I would have all these suggestions come from the President direct."

"The President!" exclaimed Gordon; "but how? what does the President know or care about Opeki? and it would take so long — oh, I see, the cable. Is that what you have been doing?" he asked.

"Well, only once," said Stedman, guiltily; "that was when he wanted to turn me out of the consul's office, and I had a cable that very afternoon, from the President, ordering me to stay where I was. Ollypybus doesn't understand the cable, of course, but he knows that it sends messages; and sometimes I pretend to send messages for him to the President; but he began asking me to tell the President to come and pay him a visit, and I had to stop it."

"I'm glad you told me," said Gordon. "The President shall begin to cable tomorrow. He will need an extra appropriation from Congress to pay for his private cablegrams alone."

"And there's another thing," said Stedman. "In all your plans, you've arranged for the people's improvement, but not for their amusement; and they are a peaceful, jolly, simple sort of people, and we must please them."

"Have they no games or amusements of their own?" asked Gordon.

"Well, not what we would call games."

"Very well, then, I'll teach them base-ball. Foot-ball would be too warm. But that plaza in front of the King's bungalow, where his palace is going to be, is just the place for a diamond. On the whole, though," added the consul, after a moment's reflection, "you'd better attend to that yourself. I don't think it becomes my dignity as American consul, to take off my coat and give lessons to young Opekians in sliding to bases; do you? No; I think you'd better do that. The Bradleys will help you, and you had better begin to-morrow. You have been wanting to know what a secretary of legation's duties are, and now you know. It's to organize base-ball nines. And after you get yours ready," he added, as he turned into his room for the night, "I'll train one that will sweep yours off the face of the island. For *this* American consul can pitch three curves."

The best-laid plans of men go far astray, sometimes, and the great and beautiful city that was to rise on the coast of Opeki was not built in a day. Nor was it ever built. For before the Bradleys could mark out the foul-lines for the base-ball field on the plaza, or teach their standing army the goose step, or lay bamboo pipes for the water-mains, or clear away the cactus for the extension of the King's palace, the Hillmen paid Opeki their quarterly visit.

Albert had called on the King the next morning, with Stedman as his interpreter, as he had said he would, and with maps and sketches, had shown his Majesty what he proposed to do towards improving Opeki and ennobling her king, and when the King saw Albert's free-hand sketches of wharves with tall ships lying at anchor, and rows of Opekian warriors with the Bradleys at their head, and the design for his new palace, and a royal sedan chair, he believed that these things were already his, and not still only on paper, and he appointed Albert his Prime Minister of War, Stedman his Minister of Home Affairs, and selected two of his wisest and oldest subjects to serve them as joint advisers. His enthusiasm was even greater than Gordon's, because he did not appreciate the difficulties. He thought Gordon a semigod, a worker of miracles, and urged the putting up of a monument to him at once in the public plaza, to which Albert objected, on the ground that it would be too suggestive of an idol; and to which Stedman also objected, but for the less unselfish reason that it would "be in the way of the pitcher's box."

They were feverishly discussing all these great changes, and Stedman was translating as rapidly as he could translate, the speeches of four different men, — for the two counsellors had been called in, all of whom wanted to speak at once, — when there came from outside, a great shout, and the screams of women, and the clashing of iron, and the pattering footsteps of men running.

As they looked at one another in startled surprise, a native ran into the room, followed by Bradley, Jr., and threw himself down before the King. While he talked, beating his hands and bowing before Ollypybus, Bradley, Jr., pulled his forelock to the consul, and told how this man lived on the far outskirts of the village; how he had been captured while out hunting, by a number of the Hillmen; and how he had escaped to tell the people that their old enemies were on the war path again, and rapidly approaching the village.

Outside, the women were gathering in the plaza, with the children about them, and the men were running from hut to hut, warning their fellows, and arming themselves with spears and swords, and the native bows and arrows.

"They might have waited until we had that army trained," said Gordon, in a tone of the keenest displeasure. "Tell me, quick, what do they generally do when they come?"

"Steal all the cattle and goats, and a woman or two, and set fire to the huts in the outskirts," replied Stedman.

"Well, we must stop them," said Gordon, jumping up. "We must take out a flag of truce and treat with them. They must be kept off until I have my army in working order. It is most inconvenient. If they had only waited two months, now, or six weeks even, we could have done something; but now we must make peace. Tell the King we are going out to fix things with them, and tell him to keep off his warriors until he learns whether we succeed or fail.

"But, Gordon!" gasped Stedman. "Albert! You don't understand. Why, man, this isn't a street fight or a cane rush. They'll stick you full of spears, dance on your body, and eat you, maybe. A flag of truce! — you're talking nonsense. What do they know of a flag of truce?"

"You're talking nonsense, too," said Albert, "and you're talking to your superior officer. If you are not with me in this, go back to your cable, and tell the man in Octavia that it's a warm day, and that the sun is shining; but if you've any spirit in you,—and I think you have,—run to the office and get my Winchester rifles, and the two shot-guns, and my revolvers, and my uniform, and a lot of brass things for presents, and run all the way there and back. And make time. Play you're riding a bicycle at the Agricultural Fair."

Stedman did not hear this last; for he was already off and away, pushing through the crowd, and calling on Bradley, Sr., to follow him. Bradley, Jr., looked at Gordon with eyes that snapped like a dog that is waiting for his master to throw a stone.

"I can fire a Winchester, sir," he said. "Old Tom can't. He's no good at long range 'cept with a big gun, sir. Don't give him the Winchester. Give it to me, please, sir."

Albert met Stedman in the plaza, and pulled off his blazer, and put on Captain Travis's—now his—uniform coat, and his white pith helmet.

"Now, Jack," he said, "get up there and tell these people that we are going out to make peace with these Hillmen, or bring them back prisoners of war. Tell them we are the preservers of their homes and wives and children; and you, Bradley, take these presents, and young Bradley, keep close to me, and carry this rifle."

Stedman's speech was hot and wild enough to suit a critical and feverish audience before a barricade in Paris. And when he was through, Gordon and Bradley punctuated his oration by firing off the two Winchester rifles in the air, at which the people jumped and fell on their knees, and prayed to their several gods. The fighting men of the village followed the four white men to the outskirts, and took up their stand there as Stedman told them to, and the four walked on over the roughly hewn road, to meet the enemy.

Gordon walked with Bradley, Jr., in advance. Stedman and old Tom Bradley followed close behind, with the two shotguns, and the presents in a basket.

"Are these Hillmen used to guns?" asked Gordon. Stedman said no, they were not.

"This shot-gun of mine is the only one on the island," he explained, "and we never came near enough them, before, to do anything with it. It only carries a hundred yards. The Opekians never make any show of resistance. They are quite content if the Hillmen satisfy themselves with the outlying huts, as long as they leave them and the town alone; so they seldom come to close quarters."

The four men walked on for a quarter of an hour or so, in silence, peering eagerly on every side; but it was not until they had left the woods and marched out into the level stretch of grassy country, that they came upon the enemy. The Hillmen were about forty in number, and were as savage and ugly-looking giants as any in a picture book. They had captured a dozen cows and goats, and were driving them on before them, as they advanced further upon the village. When they saw the four men, they gave a mixed chorus of cries and yells, and some of them stopped, and others ran forward, shaking their spears, and shooting their broad arrows into the ground before them. A tall, gray-bearded, muscular old man, with a skirt of feathers about him, and necklaces of bones and animals' claws around his bare chest, ran in front of them, and seemed to be trying to make them approach more slowly.

"Is that Messenwah?" asked Gordon.

"Yes," said Stedman; "he is trying to keep them back. I don't believe he ever saw a white man before."

"Stedman," said Albert, speaking quickly, "give your gun to Bradley, and go forward with your arms in the air, and waving your handkerchief, and tell them in their language that the King is coming. If they go at you, Bradley and I will kill a goat or two, to show them what we can do with the rifles; and if that don't stop them, we will shoot at their legs; and if that don't stop them — I guess you'd better come back, and we'll all run."

Stedman looked at Albert, and Albert looked at Stedman, and neither of them winced or flinched.

"Is this another of my secretary's duties?" asked the younger boy.

"Yes," said the consul; "but a resignation is always in order. You needn't go if you don't like it. You see, you know the language and I don't, but I know how to shoot, and you don't."

"That's perfectly satisfactory," said Stedman, handing his gun to old Bradley. "I only wanted to know why I was to be sacrificed, instead of one of the Bradleys. It's because I know the language. Bradley, Sr., you see the evil results of a higher education.

"About time to begin on the goats!"

Wish me luck, please," he said, "and for goodness' sake," he added impressively, "don't waste much time shooting goats."

The Hillmen had stopped about two hundred yards off, and were drawn up in two lines, shouting, and dancing, and hurling taunting remarks at their few adversaries. The stolen cattle were bunched together back of the King. As Stedman walked steadily forward with his handkerchief fluttering, and howling out something in their own tongue, they stopped and listened. As he advanced, his three companions followed him at about fifty yards in the rear. He was one hundred and fifty yards from the Hillmen, before they made out what he said, and then one of the young braves, resenting it as an insult to his chief, shot an arrow at him. Stedman dodged the arrow, and stood his ground without even taking a step backwards, only turning slightly to put his hands to his mouth, and to shout something which sounded to his companions like, "About time to begin on the goats." But the instant the young man had fired, King Messenwah swung his club and knocked him down, and none of the others moved. Then Messenwah advanced before his men to meet

Stedman, and on Stedman's opening and shutting his hands to show that he was unarmed, the King threw down his club and spears, and came forward as empty-handed as himself.

"Ah," gasped Bradley, Jr., with his finger trembling on his lever, "let me take a shot at him now." Gordon struck the man's gun up, and walked forward in all the glory of his gold and blue uniform; for both he and Stedman saw now that Messenwah was more impressed by their appearance, and in the fact that they were white men, than with any threats of immediate war. So when he saluted Gordon haughtily, that young man gave him a haughty nod in return, and bade Stedman tell the King that he would permit him to sit down. The King did not quite appear to like this, but he sat down, nevertheless, and nodded his head gravely.

"Now tell him," said Gordon, "that I come from the ruler of the greatest nation on earth, and that I recognize Ollypybus as the only King of this island, and that I come to this little three-penny King with either peace and presents, or bullets and war."

"Have I got to tell him he's a little

three-penny King?" said Stedman, plaintively.

"No; you needn't give a literal translation; it can be as free as you please."

"Thanks," said the secretary, humbly.

"And tell him," continued Gordon, "that we will give presents to him and his warriors if he keeps away from Ollypybus, and agrees to keep away always. If he won't do that, try to get him to agree to stay away for three months at least, and by that time we can get word to San Francisco, and have a dozen muskets over here in two months; and when our time of probation is up, and he and his merry men come dancing down the hillside, we will blow them up as high as his mountains. But you needn't tell him that, either. And if he is proud and haughty, and would rather fight, ask him to restrain himself until we show what we can do with our weapons at two hundred yards."

Stedman seated himself in the long grass in front of the King, and with many revolving gestures of his arms, and much pointing at Gordon, and profound nods and bows, retold what Gordon had dictated. When he had finished, the King looked at the bundle of presents, and at the guns, of which Stedman had given a very wonderful account, but answered nothing.

"I guess," said Stedman, with a sigh, "that we will have to give him a little practical demonstration to help matters. I am sorry, but I think one of those goats has got to die. It's like vivisection. The lower order of animals have to suffer for the good of the higher."

"Oh," said Bradley, Jr., cheerfully, "I'd just as soon shoot one of those niggers as one of the goats."

So Stedman bade the King tell his men to drive a goat towards them, and the King did so, and one of the men struck one of the goats with his spear, and it ran clumsily across the plain.

"Take your time, Bradley," said Gordon. "Aim low, and if you hit it, you can have it for supper."

"And if you miss it," said Stedman, gloomily, "Messenwah may have us for supper."

The Hillmen had seated themselves a hundred yards off, while the leaders were debating, and they now rose curiously and watched Bradley, as he sank upon one knee, and covered the goat with his rifle. When it was about one hundred and fifty yards off, he fired, and the goat fell over dead.

And then all the Hillmen, with the King himself, broke away on a run, towards the dead animal, with much shouting. The King came back alone, leaving his people standing about and examining the goat. He was much excited, and talked and gesticulated violently.

"He says—" said Stedman; "He says—"

"What? yes; go on."

"He says — goodness me! — what do you think he says?"

"Well, what does he say?" cried Gordon, in a great state of nerves. "Don't keep it all to yourself."

"He says," said Stedman, "that we are deceived. That he is no longer King of the Island of Opeki, that he is in great fear of us, and that he has got himself into no end of trouble. He says he sees that we are indeed mighty men, that to us he is as helpless as the wild boar before the javelin of the hunter."

"Well, he's right." said Gordon. "Go on."

"But that which we ask is no longer his to give. He has sold his kingship and his right to this island to another king, who came to him two days ago in a great canoe, and who made noises as we do, — with guns, I suppose he means, — and to whom he sold the island for a watch that he has in a bag around his neck. And that he signed a paper, and made marks on a piece of bark, to show that he gave up the island freely and forever."

"What does he mean?" said Gordon. "How can he give up the island. Ollypybus is the king of half of it, anyway, and he knows it."

"That's just it," said Stedman. "That's what frightens him. He said he didn't care about Ollypybus, and didn't count him in when he made the treaty, because he is such a peaceful chap that he knew he could thrash him into doing anything he wanted him to do. And now that you have turned up and taken Ollypybus's part, he wishes he hadn't sold the island, and wishes to know if you are angry."

"Angry? of course I'm angry," said Gordon, glaring as grimly at the frightened monarch as he thought was safe. "Who wouldn't be angry? Who do you think these people were who made a fool of him, Stedman? Ask him to let us see this watch."

Stedman did so, and the King fumbled among his necklaces until he had brought out a leather bag tied round his neck with a cord, and containing a plain stem-winding silver watch marked on the inside "Munich."

"That doesn't tell anything," said Gordon. "But it's plain enough. Some foreign ship of war has settled on this place as a coaling-station, or has annexed it for colonization, and they've sent a boat ashore, and they've made a treaty with this old chap, and forced him to sell his birthright for a mess of porridge. Now, that's just like those monarchical pirates; imposing upon a poor old black."

Old Bradley looked at him impudently.

"Not at all," said Gordon; "it's quite different with us; we don't want to rob him or Ollypybus, or to annex their land. All we want to do is to improve it, and have the fun of running it for them and meddling in their affairs of state. Well, Stedman," he said, "what shall we do?"

Stedman said that the best and only thing to do was to threaten to take the watch away from Messenwah, but to give him a revolver instead, which would make a friend of him for life, and to keep him supplied with cartridges only as long as he behaved himself, and then to make him understand that as Ollypybus had not given his consent to the loss of the island, Messenwah's agreement, or treaty, or whatever it was, did not stand, and that he had better come down the next day, early in the morning, and join in a general consultation. This was done, and Messenwah agreed willingly to their proposition, and was given his revolver and shown how to shoot it, while the other presents were distributed among the other men, who were as happy over them as girls with a full dance-card.

"And now, to-morrow," said Stedman, "understand, you are all to come down unarmed, and sign a treaty with great Ollypybus, in which he will agree to keep to one half of the island, if you keep to yours, and there must be no more wars or goat stealing, or this gentleman on my right and I will come up and put holes in you just as the gentleman on the left did with the goat."

Messenwah and his warriors promised to come early, and saluted reverently as Gordon and his three companions walked up together very proudly and stiffly.

"Do you know how I feel?" said Gordon.

"How?" asked Stedman.

"I feel as I used to do in the city, when the boys in the street were throwing snow-balls, and I had to go by with a high hat on my head and pretend not to know they were behind me. I always felt a cold chill down my spinal column, and I could feel that snow-ball, whether it came or not, right in the small of my back. And I can feel one of those men pulling his bow, now, and the arrow sticking out of my right shoulder."

"Oh, no, you can't," said Stedman. "They are too afraid of those rifles. But I do feel sorry for any of those warriors whom old man Massenwah doesn't like, now that he has that revolver. He isn't the sort to practise on goats."

There was great rejoicing when Stedman and Gordon told their story to the King, and the people learned they were not to have their huts burned and their cattle stolen. The armed Opekians formed a guard around the ambassadors and escorted them to their homes with cheers and shouts, and the women ran at their side and tried to kiss Gordon's hand.

"I'm sorry I can't speak the language, Stedman," said Gordon, "or I would tell them what a brave man you are. You are too modest to do it yourself, even if I dictated something for you to say. As for me," he said, pulling off his uniform, "I am thoroughly disgusted and disappointed. It never occurred to me until it was all over, that this was my chance to be a war correspondent. It wouldn't have been much of a war, but then I would have been the only one on the spot, and that counts for a great deal. Still, my time may come."

"We have a great deal on hand for to-morrow," said Gordon that evening, "and we had better turn in early."

And so the people were still singing and rejoicing down in the village, when the two conspirators for the peace of the country went to sleep for the night. It seemed to Gordon as though he had hardly turned his pillow twice to get the coolest side, when some one touched him, and he saw, by the light of the dozen glowworms in the tumbler by his bedside, a tall figure at its foot.

"It's me — Bradley," said the figure.

"Yes," said Gordon, with the haste of a man to show that sleep has no hold on him; "exactly; what is it?"

"There is a ship of war in the harbor," said Bradley, in a whisper. "I heard her anchor chains rattle when she came to, and that woke me. I could hear that if I were dead. And then I made sure by her lights; she's a great boat, sir, and I can know she's a ship of war by the challenging, when they change the watch. I thought you'd like to know, sir."

Gordon sat up and clutched his knees with his hands. "Yes, of course," he said; "you are quite right. Still, I don't see what there is to do."

He did not wish to show too much youthful interest, but though fresh from civilization, he had learnt how far from it he was, and he was curious to see this sign of it that had come so much more quickly than he had anticipated.

"Wake Mr. Stedman, will you?" said he, "and we will go and take a look at her."

"You can see nothing but the lights," said Bradley, as he left the room; "it's a black night, sir."

Stedman was not new from the sight of men and ships of war, and came in half dressed and eager.

"Do you suppose it's the big canoe Messenwah spoke of?" he said.

"I thought of that," said Gordon.

The three men fumbled their way down the road to the plaza, and saw, as soon as they turned into it, the great outlines and the brilliant lights of an immense vessel, still more immense in the darkness, and glowing like a strange monster of the sea, with just a suggestion here and there, where the lights spread, of her cabins and bridges. As they stood on the shore, shivering in the cool night wind, they heard the bells strike over the water.

"It's two o'clock," said Bradley, counting.

"Well, we can do nothing, and they cannot mean to do much to-night," Albert said. "We had better get some more sleep, and, Bradley, you keep watch and tell us as soon as day breaks."

"Aye, aye, sir," said the sailor.

"If that's the man-of-war that made the treaty with Messenwah, and Messenwah turns up to-morrow, it looks as if our day would be pretty well filled up," said Albert, as they felt their way back to the darkness.

"What do you intend to do?" asked his secretary, with a voice of some concern.

"I don't know," Albert answered gravely, from the blackness of the night. "It looks as if we were getting ahead just a little too fast; doesn't it? Well," he added, as they reached the house, "let's try to keep in step with the procession, even if we can't be drum-majors and walk in front of it." And with this cheering tone of confidence in their ears, the two diplomats went soundly asleep again.

The light of the rising sun filled the room, and the parrots were chattering outside, when Bradley woke him again.

"They are sending a boat ashore, sir," he said excitedly, and filled with the importance of the occasion. "She's a German man-of-war, and one of the new model. A beautiful boat, sir; for her lines were laid in Glasgow, and I can tell that, no matter what flag she flies. You had best be moving to meet them: the village isn't awake yet."

Albert took a cold bath and dressed leisurely; then he made Bradley, Jr., who had slept through it all, get up breakfast, and the two young men ate it and drank their coffee comfortably and with an air of confidence that deceived their servants, if it did not deceive themselves. But when they came down the path, smoking and swinging their sticks, and turned into the plaza, their composure left them like a mask, and they stopped where they stood. The plaza was enclosed by the natives gathered in whispering groups, and depressed by fear and wonder. On one side were crowded all the Messenwah warriors, unarmed, and as silent and disturbed as the Opekians. In the middle of the plaza some twenty sailors were busily rearing and bracing a tall flag-staff that they had shaped from a royal palm, and they did this as unconcernedly and as contemptuously, and with as much indifference to the strange groups on either side of them, as though they were working on a barren coast, with nothing but the startled sea-gulls about them. As Albert and Stedman came upon the scene, the flag-pole was in place, and the halliards hung from it with a little bundle of bunting at the end of one of them.

"We must find the King at once," said Gordon. He was terribly excited and angry. "It is easy enough to see what this means. They are going through the form of annexing this island to the other lands of the German government. They are robbing old Ollypybus of what is his. They have not even given him a silver watch for it."

The King was in his bungalow, facing the plaza. Messenwah was with him, and an equal number of each of their councils. The common danger had made them lie down together in peace; but they gave a gasp of relief as Gordon strode into the room with no ceremony, and greeted them with a curt wave of the hand.

"Now then, Stedman, be quick," he said. "Explain to them what this means; tell them that I will protect them; that I am anxious to see that Ollypybus is not cheated; that we will do all we can for them."

Outside, on the shore, a second boat's crew had landed a group of officers and a file of marines. They walked in all the dignity of full dress across the plaza to the flag-pole, and formed in line on the three sides of it, with the marines facing the sea. The officers, from the captain with a prayer book in his hand, to the youngest middy, were as indifferent to the frightened natives about them as the other men had been. The natives, awed and afraid, crouched back among their huts, the marines and the sailors kept their eyes front, and the German captain opened his prayer book. The debate in the bungalow was over.

"If you only had your uniform, sir," said Bradley, Sr., miserably.

"This is a little bit too serious for uniforms and bicycle medals," said Gordon. "And these men are used to gold lace."

He pushed his way through the natives, and stepped confidently across the plaza. The youngest middy saw him coming, and nudged the one next him with his elbow, and he nudged the next, but none of the officers moved, because the captain had begun to read.

"One minute, please," called Gordon.

He stepped out into the hollow square formed by the marines, and raised his helmet to the captain.

"Do you speak English or French?" Gordon said in French; "I do not understand German."

The captain lowered the book in his hands and gazed reflectively at Gordon through his spectacles, and made no reply.

"If I understand this," said the younger man, trying to be very impressive and polite, "you are laying claim to this land, in behalf of the German government."

The captain continued to observe him thoughtfully, and then said, "That iss so," and then asked, "Who are you?"

"I represent the King of this island, Ollypybus, whose people you see around you. I also represent the United States government that does not tolerate a foreign power near her coast, since the days of President Monroe and before. The treaty you have made with Messenwah is an absurdity. There is only one king with whom to treat, and he—"

The captain turned to one of his officers and said something, and then, after giving another curious glance at Gordon, raised his book and continued reading, in a deep, unruffled monotone. The officer whispered an order, and two of the marines stepped out of line, and dropping the muzzles of their muskets, pushed Gordon back out of the en-

closure, and left him there with his lips
white, and trembling all over with indignation. He would have liked to have rushed
back into the lines and broken the captain's
spectacles over his sun-tanned nose and
cheeks, but he was quite sure this would
only result in his getting shot, or in his
being made ridiculous before the natives, and
that was almost as bad, so he stood still for a
moment, with his blood choking him, and
then turned and walked back where the King
and Stedman were whispering together. Just
as he turned, one of the men pulled the
halliards, the ball of bunting ran up into the
air, bobbed, twitched, and turned, and broke
into the folds of the German flag. At the
same moment the marines raised their muskets and fired a volley, and the officers saluted
and the sailors cheered.

"Do you see that?" cried Stedman, catching
Gordon's humor, to Ollypybus; "that means
that you are no longer king, that strange
people are coming here to take your land,
and to turn your people into servants, and to
drive you back into the mountains. Are
you going to submit? are you going to let
that flag stay where it is?"

Messenwah and Ollypybus gazed at one another with fearful, helpless eyes. "We are afraid," Ollypybus cried; "we do not know what we should do."

"What do they say?" asked Gordon.

"They say they do not know what to do."

"I know what I'd do," cried Gordon. "If I were not an American consul, I'd pull down their old flag, and put a hole in their boat and sink her."

"Well, I'd wait until they get under way, before you do either of those things," said Stedman soothingly. "That captain seems to be a man of much determination of character."

"But I will pull it down," cried Gordon. "I will resign, as Travis did. I am no longer consul. You can be consul if you want to. I promote you. I am going up a step higher. I mean to be king. Tell those two," he ran on excitedly, "that their only course and only hope is in me; that they must make me ruler of the island until this thing is over; that I will resign again as soon as it is settled, but that some one must act at once, and if they are afraid to, I am not, only they must give me authority to act for them. They must abdicate in my favor."

"Are you in earnest?" gasped Stedman.

"Don't I talk as if I was?" demanded Gordon, wiping the perspiration from his forehead.

"And can I be consul?" said Stedman, cheerfully.

"Of course. Tell them what I propose to do."

Stedman turned and spoke rapidly to the two kings. The people gathered closer to hear.

The two rival monarchs looked at one another in silence for a moment, and then both began to speak at once, their consulars interrupting them and mumbling their guttural comments with anxious earnestness. It did not take them very long to see that they were all of one mind, and then they both turned to Gordon and dropped on one knee, and placed his hands on their foreheads, and Stedman raised his cap.

"They agree," he explained, for it was but pantomime to Albert. "They salute you as a ruler; they are calling you Tellaman, which means peacemaker. The Peacemaker, that is your title. I hope you will deserve it, but I think they might have chosen a more appropriate one."

"Then I'm really King?" demanded Albert, decidedly, "and I can do what I please? They give me full power. Quick, do they?"

"Yes, but don't do it," begged Stedman, "and just remember I am American consul now, and that is a much superior being to a crowned monarch; you said so yourself."

Albert did not reply to this, but ran across the plaza followed by the two Bradleys. The boats had gone.

"Hoist that flag beside the brass cannon," he cried, "and stand ready to salute it when I drop this one."

Bradley, Jr., grasped the halliards of the flag, which he had forgotten to raise and salute in the morning in all the excitement of the man-of-war's arrival. Bradley, Sr., stood by the brass cannon, blowing gently on his lighted fuse. The Peacemaker took the halliards of the German flag in his two hands, gave a quick, sharp tug, and down came the red, white, and black piece of bunting, and the next moment young Bradley sent the stars and stripes up in their place. As it rose, Bradley's brass cannon barked merrily like a little bull-dog, and the Peacemaker cheered.

"Why don't you cheer, Stedman?" he shouted. "Tell those people to cheer for all they are worth. What sort of an American consul are you?"

Stedman raised his arm half-heartedly to give the time, and opened his mouth; but his arm remained fixed and his mouth open, while his eyes stared at the retreating boat of the German man-of-war. In the stern sheets of this boat, the stout German captain was struggling unsteadily to his feet; he raised his arm and waved it to some one on the great man-of-war, as though giving an order. The natives looked from Stedman to the boat, and even Gordon stopped in his cheering and stood motionless, watching. They had not very long to wait. There was a puff of white smoke, and a flash, and then a loud report, and across the water came a great black ball skipping lightly through and over the waves, as easily as a flat stone thrown by a boy. It seemed to come very slowly. At least it came slowly enough for every one to see that it was coming directly towards the brass cannon. The Bradleys saw this certainly, for they ran as fast as they could, and kept on running. The ball caught the cannon under its mouth, and tossed it in the air, knocking the flag-pole into a dozen pieces, and passing on through two of the palm-covered huts.

"Great Heavens, Gordon!" cried Stedman; "they are firing on us."

But Gordon's face was radiant and wild.

"Firing on *us!*" he cried. "On *us!* Don't you see? Don't you understand? What do *we* amount to? They have fired on the American flag. Don't you see what that means? It means war. A great international war. And I am a war correspondent at last!" He ran up to Stedman and seized him by the arm so tightly that it hurt.

"By three o'clock," he said, "they will know in the office what has happened. The country will know it to-morrow when the paper is on the street; people will read it all over the world. The Emperor will hear of it at breakfast; the President will cable for further particulars. He will get them. It is the chance of a lifetime, and we are on the spot."

Stedman did not hear this; he was watching the broadside of the ship to see another puff of white smoke, but there came no such sign. The two row-boats were raised, there was a cloud of black smoke from the funnel, a creaking of chains sounding faintly across the water, and the ship started at half speed and moved out of the harbor. The Opekians and the Hillmen fell on their knees, or to dancing, as best suited their sense of relief, but Gordon shook his head.

"They are only going to land the marines," he said; "perhaps they are going to the spot they stopped at before, or to take up another position further out at sea. They will land men and then shell the town, and the land forces will march here and co-operate with the vessel, and everybody will be taken prisoner or killed. We have the centre of the stage, and we are making history."

"I'd rather read it than make it," said Stedman. "You've got us in a senseless, silly position, Gordon, and a mighty unpleasant one. And for no reason that I can see, except to make copy for your paper."

"Tell those people to get their things together," said Gordon, "and march back out of danger into the woods. Tell Ollypybus I am going to fix things all right; I don't know just how yet, but I will, and now come after me as quickly as you can to the cable office. I've got to tell the paper all about it."

It was three o'clock before the "chap at Octavia" answered Stedman's signalling. Then Stedman delivered Gordon's message, and immediately shut off all connection, before the Octavia operator could question him. Gordon dictated his message in this way: —

"Begin with the date line, 'Opeki, June 22.'

"At seven o'clock this morning, the captain and officers of the German man-of-war *Kaiser*, went through the ceremony of annexing this island in the name of the German Emperor, basing their right to do so on an agreement made with a leader of a wandering tribe, known as the Hillmen. King Ollypybus, the present monarch of Opeki, delegated his authority, as also did the leader of the Hillmen, to King Tallaman, or the Peacemaker, who tore down the German flag, and raised that of the United States in its place. At the same moment the flag was saluted by the battery. This salute, being mistaken for an attack on the *Kaiser*, was answered by that vessel. Her first shot took immediate effect, completely destroying the entire battery of the Opekians, cutting down the American flag, and destroying the houses of the people —"

"There was only one brass cannon and two huts," expostulated Stedman.

"Well, that was the whole battery, wasn't it?" asked Gordon, "and two huts is plural. I said houses of the people. I couldn't say two house of the people. Just you send this as you get it. You are not an American consul at the present moment. You are an under-paid agent of a cable company, and you send my stuff as I write it. The American residents have taken refuge in the consulate — that's us," explained Gordon, "and the English residents have sought refuge in the woods — that's the Bradleys. King Tellaman — that's me — declares his intention of fighting against the annexation. The forces of the Opekians are under the command of Captain Thomas Bradley — I guess I might as well made him a colonel — of Colonel Thomas Bradley, of the English army.

"'The American consul says — Now, what do you say, Stedman? Hurry up, please," asked Gordon, "and say something good and strong."

"You get me all mixed up," complained Stedman, plaintively. "Which am I now, a cable operator or the American consul?"

"Consul, of course. Say something patriotic and about your determination to protect the interests of your government, and all that." Gordon bit the end of his pencil impatiently, and waited.

"I won't be anything of the sort, Gordon," said Stedman; "you are getting me into an awful lot of trouble, and yourself too. I won't say a word."

"The American consul," read Gordon, as his pencil wriggled across the paper, "refuses to say anything for publication until he has communicated with the authorities at Washington, but from all I can learn he sympathizes entirely with Tellaman. Your correspondent has just returned from an audience with King Tellaman, who asks him to inform the American people that the Monroe doctrine will be sustained as long as he rules this island. I guess that's enough to begin with," said Gordon. "Now send that off quick, and then get away from the instrument before the man in Octavia begins to ask questions. I am going out to precipitate matters."

Gordon found the two kings sitting dejectedly side by side, and gazing grimly upon the disorder of the village, from which the people were taking their leave as quickly as they could get their few belongings piled upon the ox-carts. Gordon walked amongst them, helping them in every way he could, and tasting, in their subservience and gratitude, the sweets of sovereignty. When Stedman had locked up the cable office and rejoined him, he bade him tell Messenwah to send three of his youngest men and fastest runners back to the hills to watch for the German vessel and see where she was attempting to land her marines.

"This is a tremendous chance for descriptive writing, Stedman," said Gordon, enthusiastically, "all this confusion and excitement, and the people leaving their homes and all that. It's like the people getting out of Brussels before Waterloo, and then the scene at the foot of the mountains, while they are camping out there, until the Germans leave. I never had a chance like this before."

It was quite dark by six o'clock, and none of the three messengers had as yet returned.

Gordon walked up and down the empty plaza and looked now at the horizon for the man-of-war, and again down the road back of the village. But neither the vessel nor the messengers, bearing word of her, appeared. The night passed without any incident, and in the morning Gordon's impatience became so great that he walked out to where the villagers were in camp and passed on half way up the mountain, but he could see no sign of the man-of-war. He came back more restless than before, and keenly disappointed.

"If something don't happen before three o'clock, Stedman," he said, "our second cablegram will have to consist of glittering generalities and a lengthy interview with King Tellaman, by himself."

Nothing did happen. Ollypybus and Messenwah began to breathe more freely. They believed the new king had succeeded in frightening the German vessel away forever. But the new king upset their hopes by telling them that the Germans had undoubtedly already landed, and had probably killed the three messengers.

"Now, then," he said, with pleased expectation, as Stedman and he seated themselves in the cable office at three o'clock, "open it up and let's find out what sort of an impression we have made."

Stedman's face, as the answer came in to his first message of greeting, was one of strangely marked disapproval.

"What does he say?" demanded Gordon, anxiously.

"He hasn't done anything but swear yet," answered Stedman, grimly.

"What is he swearing about?"

"He wants to know why I left the cable yesterday. He says he has been trying to call me up for the last twenty-four hours. Ever since I sent my message at three o'clock. The home office is jumping mad, and want me discharged. They won't do that, though," he said, in a cheerful aside, "because they haven't paid me my salary for the last eight months. He says — great Scott! this will please you, Gordon — he says there have been over two hundred queries for matter from papers all over the United States, and from Europe. Your paper beat them on the news, and now the home office is packed with San Francisco reporters, and the telegrams are coming in every minute, and they have been abusing him for not answering them, and he says that I'm a fool. He wants as much as you can send, and all the details. He says all the papers will have to put 'By Yokohama Cable Company' on the top of each message they print, and that that is advertising the company, and is sending the stock up. It rose fifteen points on 'change in San Francisco to-day, and the president and the other officers—"

"Oh, I don't want to hear about their old company," snapped out Gordon, pacing up and down in despair. "What am I to do? that's what I want to know. Here I have the whole country stirred up and begging for news. On their knees for it, and a cable all to myself and the only man on the spot, and nothing to say. I'd just like to know how long that German idiot intends to wait before he begins shelling this town and killing people. He has put me in a most absurd position."

"Here's a message for you, Gordon," said Stedman, with business-like calm. "Albert Gordon, Correspondent," he read: "Try American consul. First message O.K.; beat the country; can take all you send. Give names of foreign residents massacred, and fuller account blowing up palace. Dodge."

The expression on Gordon's face as this message was slowly read off to him, had changed from one of gratified pride to one of puzzled consternation.

"What's he mean by foreign residents massacred, and blowing up of palace?" asked Stedman, looking over his shoulder anxiously. "Who is Dodge?"

"Dodge is the night editor," said Gordon, nervously. "They must have read my message wrong. You sent just what I gave you, didn't you?" he asked.

"Of course I did," said Stedman, indignantly.

"I didn't say anything about the massacre of anybody, did I?" asked Gordon. "I hope they are not improving on my account. What *am* I to do? This is getting awful. I'll have to go out and kill a few people myself. Oh, why don't that Dutch captain begin to do something! What sort of a fighter does he call himself? He wouldn't shoot at a school of porpoises. He's not—"

"Here comes a message to Leonard T.

Travis, American consul, Opeki," read Stedman. "It's raining messages to-day. 'Send full details of massacre of American citizens by German sailors.' Secretary of — great Scott!" gasped Stedman, interrupting himself and gazing at his instrument with horrified fascination — "the Secretary of State."

"That settles it," roared Gordon, pulling at his hair and burying his face in his hands. "I have *got* to kill some of them now."

"Albert Gordon, Correspondent," read Stedman, impressively, like the voice of Fate. "Is Colonel Thomas Bradley commanding native forces at Opeki, Colonel Sir Thomas Kent-Bradley of Crimean war fame? Correspondent London *Times*, San Francisco Press Club."

"Go on, go on!" said Gordon, desperately. "I'm getting used to it now. Go on!"

"American consul, Opeki," read Stedman. "Home Secretary desires you to furnish list of names English residents killed during shelling of Opeki by ship of war *Kaiser*, and estimate of amount property destroyed. Stoughton, Office of English consul, San Francisco."

"Stedman!" cried Gordon, jumping to his feet, "there's a mistake here somewhere. These people cannot all have made my message read like that. Some one has altered it, and now I have got to make these people here live up to that message, whether they like being massacred and blown up or not. Don't answer any of those messages, except the one from Dodge; tell him things have quieted down a bit, and that I'll send four thousand words on the flight of the natives from the village, and their encampment at the foot of the mountains, and of the exploring party we have sent out to look for the German vessel; and now I am going out to make something happen."

Gordon said he would be gone for two hours at least, and as Stedman did not feel capable of receiving any more nerve-stirring messages, he cut off all connection with Octavia, by saying, "Good by for two hours," and running away from the office. He sat down on a rock on the beach, and mopped his face with his handkerchief.

"After a man has taken nothing more exciting than weather reports from Octavia for a year," he soliloquized, "it's a bit disturbing to have all the crowned heads of Europe and their secretaries calling upon you for details of a massacre that never came off."

At the end of two hours Gordon came back from the consulate with a mass of manuscript in his hand.

"Here's three thousand words," he said desperately. "I never wrote more and said less in my life. It will made them weep at the office. I had to pretend that they knew all that had happened so far; they apparently do know more than we do, and I have filled it full of prophesies of more trouble ahead, and with interviews with myself and the two ex-Kings. The only news element in it is, that the messengers have returned to report that the German vessel is not in sight, and that there is no news. They think she has gone for good. Suppose she has, Stedman," he groaned, looking at him helplessly, "what *am* I going to do?"

"Well, as for me," said Stedman, "I'm afraid to go near that cable. It's like playing with a live wire. My nervous system won't stand many more such shocks as those they gave us this morning."

Gordon threw himself down dejectedly in

a chair in the office, and Stedman approached his instrument gingerly, as though it might explode.

"He's swearing again," he explained sadly, in answer to Gordon's look of inquiry. "He wants to know when I am going to stop running away from the wire. He has a stack of messages to send, he says, but I guess he'd better wait and take your copy first; don't you think so?"

"Yes, I do," said Gordon. "I don't want any more messages than I've had. That's the best I can do." he said, as he threw his manuscript down beside Stedman. "And they can keep on cabling until the wire burns red hot, and they won't get any more."

There was silence in the office for some time, while Stedman looked over Gordon's copy, and Gordon stared dejectedly out at the ocean.

"This is pretty poor stuff, Gordon," said Stedman. "It's like giving people milk when they want brandy."

"Don't you suppose I know that?" growled Gordon. "It's the best I can do, isn't it? It's not my fault that we are not all dead now. I can't massacre foreign residents if there are no foreign residents, but I can commit suicide though, and I'll do it if something don't happen."

There was a long pause, in which the silence of the office was only broken by the sound of the waves beating on the coral reefs outside. Stedman raised his head wearily.

"He's swearing again," he said; "he says this stuff of yours is all nonsense. He says stock in the Y. C. C. has gone up to one hundred and two, and that owners are unloading and making their fortunes, and that this sort of descriptive writing is not what the company want."

"What's he think I'm here for?" cried Gordon. "Does he think I pulled down the German flag and risked my neck half a dozen times and had myself made King just to boom his Yokohama cable stock? Confound him! You might at least swear back. Tell him just what the situation is in a few words. Here, stop that rigmarole to the paper, and explain to your home office that we are awaiting developments, and that, in the meanwhile, they must put up with the best we can send them. Wait; send this to Octavia."

Gordon wrote rapidly, and read what he wrote as rapidly as it was written.

"Operator, Octavia. You seem to have misunderstood my first message. The facts in the case are these. A German man-of-war raised a flag on this island. It was pulled down and the American flag raised in its place and saluted by a brass cannon. The German man-of-war fired once at the flag and knocked it down, and then steamed away and has not been seen since. Two huts were upset, that is all the damage done; the battery consisted of the one brass cannon before mentioned. No one, either native or foreign, has been massacred. The English residents are two sailors. The American residents are the young man who is sending you this cable and myself. Our first message was quite true in substance, but perhaps misleading in detail. I made it so because I fully expected much more to happen immediately. Nothing has happened, or seems likely to happen, and that is the exact situation up to date. Albert Gordon."

"Now," he asked after a pause, "what does he say to that?"

"He doesn't say anything," said Stedman.

"I guess he has fainted. Here it comes," he added in the same breath. He bent toward his instrument, and Gordon raised himself from his chair and stood beside him as he read it off. The two young men hardly breathed in the intensity of their interest.

"Dear Stedman," he slowly read aloud. "You and your young friend are a couple of fools. If you had allowed me to send you the messages awaiting transmission here to you, you would not have sent me such a confession of guilt as you have just done. You had better leave Opeki at once or hide in the hills. I am afraid I have placed you in a somewhat compromising position with the company, which is unfortunate, especially as, if I am not mistaken, they owe you some back pay. You should have been wiser in your day, and bought Y. C. C. stock when it was down to five cents, as yours truly did. You are not, Stedman, as bright a boy as some. And as for your friend, the war correspondent, he has queered himself for life. You see, my dear Stedman, after I had sent off your first message, and demands for further details came pouring in, and I could not get you at the wire to supply them, I took the liberty of sending some on myself."

"Great Heavens!" gasped Gordon.

Stedman grew very white under his tan, and the perspiration rolled on his cheeks.

"Your message was so general in its nature, that it allowed my imagination full play, and I sent on what I thought would please the papers, and what was much more important to me, would advertise the Y. C. C. stock. This I have been doing while waiting for material from you. Not having a clear idea of the dimensions or population of Opeki, it is possible that I have done you and your newspaper friend some injustice. I killed off about a hundred American residents, two hundred English, because I do not like the English, and a hundred French. I blew up old Ollypybus and his palace with dynamite, and shelled the city, destroying some hundred thousand dollars' worth of property, and then I waited anxiously for your friend to substantiate what I had said. This he has most unkindly failed to do. I am very sorry, but much more so for him than for myself, for I, my dear friend, have cabled on to a man in San Francisco, who is one of the directors of the Y. C. C., to sell all my stock, which he has done at one hundred and two, and he is keeping the money until I come. And I leave Octavia this afternoon to reap my just reward. I am in about $20,000 on your little war, and I feel grateful. So much so that I will inform you that the ship of war *Kaiser* has arrived at San Francisco, for which port she sailed directly from Opeki. Her captain has explained the real situation, and offered to make every amend for the accidental indignity shown to our flag. He says he aimed at the cannon, which was trained on his vessel, and which had first fired on him. But you must know, my dear Stedman, that before his arrival, war vessels belonging to the several powers mentioned in my revised dispatches, had started for Opeki at full speed, to revenge the butchery of the foreign residents. A word, my dear young friend, to the wise is sufficient. I am indebted to you to the extent of $20,000, and in return I give you this kindly advice. Leave Opeki. If there is no other way, swim. But leave Opeki."

The sun, that night, as it sank below the line where the clouds seemed to touch the sea, merged them both into a blazing, blood-red curtain, and colored the most wonderful spectacle that the natives of Opeki had ever seen. Six great ships of war, stretching out over a league of sea, stood blackly out against the red background, rolling and rising, and leaping forward, flinging back smoke and burning sparks up into the air behind them, and throbbing and panting like living creatures in their race for revenge. From the south, came a three-decked vessel, a great island of floating steel, with a flag as red as the angry sky behind it, snapping in the wind. To the south of it plunged two long low-lying torpedo boats, flying the French tri-color, and still further to the north towered three magnificent hulls of the White Squadron. Vengeance was written on every curve and line, on each straining engine rod, and on each polished gun muzzle.

And in front of these, a clumsy fishing boat rose and fell on each passing wave. Two sailors sat in the stern, holding the rope and tiller, and in the bow, with their backs turned forever toward Opeki, stood two young

To the North towered three magnificent hulls of the White Squadron.

boys, their faces lit by the glow of the setting sun and stirred by the sight of the great engines of war plunging past them on their errand of vengeance.

"Stedman," said the elder boy, in an awe-struck whisper, and with a wave of his hand, "we have not lived in vain."

MIDSUMMER PIRATES.

The boys living at the Atlantic House, and the boys boarding at Chadwick's, held mutual sentiments of something not unlike enmity — feelings of hostility from which even the older boarders were not altogether free. Nor was this unnatural under the circumstances.

When Judge Henry S. Carter and his friend Dr. Prescott first discovered Manasquan, such an institution as the Atlantic House seemed an impossibility, and land improvement companies, Queen Anne cottages, and hacks to and from the railroad station, were out of all calculation. At that time "Captain" Chadwick's farmhouse, though not rich in all the modern improvements of a seaside hotel, rejoiced in a table covered three times a day with the good things from the farm. The river back of the house was full of fish, and the pine woods along its banks were intended by nature expressly for the hanging of hammocks.

The chief amusements were picnics to the head of the river (or as near the head as the boats could get through the lily-pads), crabbing along the shore, and races on the river itself, which, if it was broad, was so absurdly shallow that an upset meant nothing more serious than a wetting and a temporary loss of reputation as a sailor.

But all this had been spoiled by the advance of civilization and the erection of the Atlantic House.

The railroad surveyors, with their high-top boots and transits, were the first signs of the approaching evils. After them came the Ozone Land Company, which bought up all the sand hills bordering on the ocean, and proceeded to stake out a flourishing "city by the sea" and to erect sign-posts in the marshes to show where they would lay out streets named after the directors of the Ozone Land Company and the Presidents of the United States.

It was not unnatural, therefore, that the Carters, and the Prescotts, and all the judge's clients, and the doctor's patients, who had been coming to Manasquan for many years, and loved it for its simplicity and quiet, should feel aggrieved at these great changes. And though the young Carters and Prescotts endeavored to impede the march of civilization by pulling up the surveyor's stakes and tearing down the Land Company's sign-posts, the inevitable improvements marched steadily on.

I hope all this will show why it was that the boys who lived at the Atlantic House — and dressed as if they were still in the city, and had "hops" every evening — were not pleasing to the boys who boarded at Chadwick's, who never changed their flannel suits for anything more formal than their bathing-dresses, and spent the summer nights on the river.

This spirit of hostility and its past history were explained to the new arrival at Chadwick's by young Teddy Carter, as the two sat under the willow tree watching a game of tennis. The new arrival had just expressed his surprise at the earnest desire manifest on the part of the entire Chadwick establishment to defeat the Atlantic House people in the great race which was to occur on the day following.

"Well, you see, sir," said Teddy, "considerable depends on this race. As it is now, we stand about even. The Atlantic House beat us playing base-ball, — though they had to get the waiters to help them, — and we beat them at tennis. Our house is great on tennis. Then we had a boat race, and our boat won. They claimed it wasn't a fair race, because their best boat was stuck on the sand bar, and so we agreed to sail it over again. The second time the wind gave out, and all the boats had to be poled home. The Atlantic House boat was poled in first, and her crew claimed the race. Wasn't it silly of them? Why, Charley Prescott told them, if they'd only said it was to be a *poling* match, he'd have entered a mud-scow and left his sail-boat at the dock!"

"And so you are going to race again tomorrow?" asked the new arrival.

"Well, it isn't exactly a race," explained Teddy. "It's a game we boys have invented. We call it 'Pirates and Smugglers.' It's something like tag, only we play it on the water, in boats. We divide boats and boys up into two sides; half of them are pirates or smugglers, and half of them are revenue officers or man-o'-war's-men. The 'Pirate's Lair' is at the island, and our dock is 'Cuba.' That's where the smugglers run in for cargoes of cigars and brandy. Mr. Moore gives us his empty cigar boxes, and Miss Sherrill (the lady who's down here for her health) let us have all the empty Apollinaris bottles. We fill the bottles with water colored with crushed blackberries, and that answers for brandy.

"The revenue officers are stationed at Annapolis (that's the Atlantic House dock), and when they see a pirate start from the island, or from our dock, they sail after him. If they can touch him with the bow of their boat, or if one of their men can board him, that counts one for the revenue officers; and they take down his sail and the pirate captain gives up his tiller as a sign of surrender.

"Then they tow him back to Annapolis, where they keep him a prisoner until he is exchanged. But if the pirate can dodge the Custom House boat, and get to the place he started for, without being caught, that counts one for him."

"Very interesting, indeed," said the new arrival; "but suppose the pirate won't be captured or give up his tiller, what then?"

"Oh, well, in that case," said Teddy, reflectively, "they'd cut his sheet-rope, or splash water on him, or hit him with an oar, or something. But he generally gives right up. Now to-morrow the Atlantic House boys are to be the revenue officers and we are to be the pirates. They have been watching us as we played the game, all summer, and they think they understand it well enough to capture our boats without any trouble at all."

"And what do you think?" asked the new arrival.

"Well, I can't say, certainly. They have faster boats than ours, but they don't know how to sail them. If we had their boats, or if they knew as much about the river as we do, it would be easy enough to name the winners. But as it is, it's about even."

Every one who owned a boat was on the river the following afternoon, and those who didn't own a boat hired or borrowed one — with or without the owner's permission.

The shore from Chadwick's to the Atlantic House dock was crowded with people. All Manasquan seemed to be ranged in line along the river's bank. Crab-men and clam-diggers mixed indiscriminately with the summer boarders; and the beach-wagons and stages from Chadwick's grazed the wheels of the dog-carts and drags from the Atlantic's livery stables.

It does not take much to overthrow the pleasant routine of summer-resort life, and the state of temporary excitement existing at the two houses on the eve of the race was not limited to the youthful contestants.

The proprietor of the Atlantic House had already announced an elaborate supper in honor of the anticipated victory, and every father and mother whose son was to take part in the day's race felt the importance of the occasion even more keenly than the son himself.

"Of course," said Judge Carter, "it's only a game, and for my part, so long as no one is drowned, I don't really care who wins; *but*, if our boys" ("our boys" meaning all three crews) "allow those young whippersnappers from the Atlantic House to win the pennant, they deserve to have their boats taken from them and exchanged for hoops and marbles!"

Which goes to show how serious a matter was the success of the Chadwick crews.

At three o'clock the amateur pirates started from the dock to take up their positions at the island. Each of the three small cat-boats, held two boys: one at the helm and one in charge of the centre-board and sheet-rope. Each pirate wore a jersey striped with differing colors, and the head of each bore the sanguinary red knitted cap, in which all genuine pirates are wont to appear. From the peaks of the three boats floated black flags, bearing the emblematic skull and bones of Captain Kidd's followers.

As they left the dock the Chadwick's people cheered with delight at their appearance and shouted encouragement, while the remaining youngsters fired salutes with a small cannon, which added to the uproar as well as increased the excitement of the moment by its likelihood to explode.

At the Atlantic House dock, also, the excitement was at fever heat.

Clad in white flannel suits and white duck yachting-caps with gilt buttons, the revenue officers strolled up and down the pier with an air of cool and determined purpose such as

Decatur may have worn as he paced the deck of his man-of-war and scanned the horizon for Algerine pirates. The stars and stripes floated bravely from the peaks of the three cat-boats, soon to leap in pursuit of the pirate craft which were conspicuously making for the starting-point at the island.

At half-past three the judge's steam-launch, the *Gracie*, made for the middle of the river, carrying two representatives from both houses and a dozen undergraduates from different colleges, who had chartered the boat for the purpose of following the race and seeing at close quarters all that was to be seen.

They enlivened the occasion by courteously and impartially giving the especial yell of each college of which there was a representative present, whether they knew him or not, or whether he happened to be an undergraduate, a professor, or an alumnus. Lest some one might inadvertently be overlooked, they continued to yell throughout the course of the afternoon, giving, in time, the shibboleth of every known institution of learning.

"Which do I think is going to win?" said the veteran boat-builder of Manasquan to

"Which do I think is going to win?" said the veteran boat-builder of M——siquan.

the inquiring group around his boat-house. "Well, I wouldn't like to say. You see, I built every one of those boats that sails to-day, and every time I make a boat I make it better than the last one. Now, the Chadwick boats I built near five years ago, and the Atlantic House boats I built last summer, and I've learned a good deal in five years."

"So you think our side will win?" eagerly interrupted an Atlantic House boarder.

"Well, I didn't say so, did I?" inquired the veteran, with crushing slowness of speech. "I didn't say so. For though these boats the Chadwick's boys have is five years old, they're good boats still; and those boys know every trick and turn of 'em — and they know every current and sand-bar just as though it was marked with a piece of chalk. So if the Atlantic folks win, it'll be because they've got the best boats; and if the Chadwick boys win, they'll win because they're better sailors."

In the fashion of all first-class aquatic contests, it was fully half an hour after the time appointed for the race to begin before the first pirate boat left the island.

The *Ripple*, with Judge Carter's two sons

in command, was the leader; and when her sail filled and showed above the shore, a cheer from the Chadwick's dock was carried to the ears of the pirate crew who sat perched on the rail as she started on her first long tack.

In a moment, two of the Atlantic House heroes tumbled into the *Osprey*, a dozen over-hasty hands had cast off her painter, had shoved her head into the stream, and the great race was begun.

The wind was down the river, or toward the island, so that while the *Osprey* was sailing before the wind, the *Ripple* had her sail close-hauled and was tacking.

"They're after us!" said Charley Carter, excitedly. "It's the *Osprey;* but I can't make out who's handling her. From the way they are pointing, I think they expect to reach us on this tack as we go about."

The crew of the *Osprey* evidently thought so too, for her bow was pointed at a spot on the shore, near which the *Ripple* must turn if she continued much longer on the same tack.

"Do you see that?" gasped Charley, who was acting as lookout. "They're letting her drift in the wind so as not to get there before us. I tell you what it is, Gus, they know what they're doing, and I think we'd better go about now."

"Do you?" inquired the younger brother, who had a lofty contempt for the other's judgment as a sailor. "Well, I don't. My plan is simply this: I am going to run as near the shore as I can, then go about sharp, and let them drift by us by a boat's length. A boat's length is as good as a mile, and then, when we are both heading the same way, I would like to see them touch us!"

"What's the use of taking such risks?" demanded the elder brother. "I tell you, we can't afford to let them get so near as that."

"At the same time," replied the man at the helm, "that is what we are going to do. I am commanding this boat, please to remember, and if I take the risks I am willing to take the blame."

"You'll be doing well, if you get off with nothing but blame," growled the elder brother. "If you let those kids catch us, I'll throw you overboard!"

"I'll put you in irons for threatening a superior officer if you don't keep quiet," answered the younger Carter, with a grin, and the mutiny ended.

It certainly would have been great sport to have run almost into the arms of the revenue officers, and then to have turned and led them a race to the goal, but the humor of young Carter's plan was not so apparent to the anxious throng of sympathizers on Chadwick's dock.

"What's the matter with the boys? Why don't they go about?" asked Captain Chadwick, excitedly. "One would think they were trying to be caught."

As he spoke, the sail of the *Ripple* fluttered in the wind, her head went about sharply, and, as her crew scrambled up on the windward rail, she bent and bowed gracefully on the homeward tack.

But, before the boat was fully under way, the *Osprey* came down upon her with a rush. The Carters hauled in the sail until their sheet lay almost flat with the surface of the river, the water came pouring over the leeward rail, and the boys threw their bodies far over the other side, in an effort to right her. The next instant there was a crash, the despised boat of the Atlantic House struck her fairly in the side, and one of the Atlantic House crew had boarded the *Ripple* with a painter in one hand and his hat in the other.

Whether it was the shock of the collision, or disgust at having been captured, no one could tell; but when the *Osprey's* bow struck the *Ripple*, the younger Carter calmly let himself go over backward and remained in the mud with the water up to his chin and without making an effort to help himself, until the judge's boat picked him up and carried him, an ignominious prisoner-of-war, to the Atlantic House dock.

The disgust over the catastrophe to the pirate crew was manifested on the part of the Chadwick sympathizers by gloomy silence or loudly expressed indignation. On the whole, it was perhaps just as well that the two Carters, as prisoners-of-war, were forced to remain at the Atlantic House dock, for their reception at home would not have been a gracious one.

Their captors, on the other hand, were received with all the honor due triumphant heroes, and were trotted off the pier on the shoulders of their cheering admirers; while the girls in the carriages waved their parasols and handkerchiefs and the colored waiters on the banks danced up and down and shouted like so many human calliopes.

The victories of John Paul Jones and the rescue of Lieutenant Greely became aquatic events of little importance in comparison. Everybody was so encouraged at this first success, that Atlantic House stock rose fifty points in as many seconds, and the next crew to sally forth from that favored party felt that the second and decisive victory was already theirs.

Again the black flag appeared around the bank of the island, and on the instant a second picked crew of the Atlantic House was in pursuit. But the boys who commanded the pirate craft had no intention of taking or giving any chances. They put their boat about, long before the revenue officers expected them to do so, and forced their adversaries to go so directly before the wind that their boat rocked violently. It was not long before the boats drew nearer together, again, as if they must certainly meet at a point not more than a hundred yards from the Atlantic House pier, where the excitement had passed the noisy point and had reached that of titillating silence.

"Go about sharp!" snapped out the captain of the pirate boat, pushing his tiller from him and throwing his weight upon it. His first officer pulled the sail close over the deck, the wind caught it fairly, and almost before the spectators were aware of it, the pirate boat had gone about and was speeding away on another tack. The revenue officers were not prepared for this. They naturally thought the pirates would run as close to the shore as they possibly could before they tacked, and were aiming for the point at which they calculated their opponents would go about, just as did the officers in the first race.

Seeing this, and not wishing to sail too close to them, the pirates had gone about much farther from the shore than was needful. In order to follow them the revenue officers were now forced to come about and tack, which, going before the wind as they were, they found less easy. The sudden change in their opponents' tactics puzzled them, and one of the two boys bungled. On future occasions each confidentially informed his friends that it was the other who was responsible; but, however that may have been, the boat missed stays, her sail flapped weakly in the breeze, and, while the crew were vigorously trying to set her in the wind by lashing the water with her rudder, the pirate boat was off and away, one hundred yards to the good, and the remainder of the race was a procession of two boats with the pirates easily in the lead.

And now came the final struggle. Now came the momentous "rubber," which was to plunge Chadwick's into gloom, or keep them still the champions of the river. The appetites of both were whetted for victory by the single triumph each had already won, and their representatives felt that, for them, success or a watery grave were the alternatives.

The Atlantic House boat, the *Wave*, and the boat upon which the Chadwick's hopes were set, the *Rover*, were evenly matched, their crews were composed of equally good sailors, and each was determined to tow the other ignominiously into port.

The two Prescotts watched the *Wave* critically and admiringly, as she came toward them with her crew perched on her side and the water showing white under her bow.

"They're coming entirely too fast to suit *me*," said the elder Prescott. "I want more room, and I have a plan to get it. Stand ready to go about." The younger brother stood ready to go about, keeping the *Rover* on her first tack until she was clear of the island's high banks and had the full sweep of the wind; then, to the surprise of her pursuers and the bewilderment of the spectators, she went smartly about, and turning her bow directly away from the goal, started before the wind back past the island and toward the wide stretch of river on the upper side.

"What's your man doing that for?" excitedly asked one of the Atlantic House people, of the prisoners-of-war.

"I don't know, certainly," one of the Carters answered; "but I suppose he thinks his boat can go faster before the wind than the *Wave* can, and he is counting on getting a long lead on her before he turns to go back. There is much more room up there, and the opportunities for dodging are about twice as good."

"Why didn't *we* think of that, Gus?" whispered the other Carter.

"We were too anxious to show what smart sailors we were, to think of anything!" answered his brother, ruefully.

Beyond the island the *Rover* gained rapidly; but as soon as she turned and began beating homeward, the *Wave* showed that tacking was her strong point and began, in turn, to make up all the advantage the *Rover* had gained.

The *Rover's* pirate-king cast a troubled eye at the distant goal and at the slowly but steadily advancing *Wave*.

His younger brother noticed the look.

"If one could only *do* something," he exclaimed, impatiently. "That's the worst of sailing races. In a rowing race you can pull till you break your back, if you want to; but here you must just sit still and watch the other fellow creep up, inch by inch, without doing anything to help yourself. If I could only get out and push, or pole! It's this trying to keep still that drives me crazy."

"I think we'd better go about now," said the commander, quietly, "and instead of going about again when we are off the bar, I intend to try to cross it."

"What!" gasped the younger Prescott, "go across the bar at low water? You can't do it. We'll stick sure. Don't try it. Don't think of it!"

"It is rather a forlorn hope, I know," said his brother; "but you can see, yourself, they're bound to overhaul us if we keep on — we don't draw as much water as they do, and if they try to follow us we'll leave them high and dry on the bar."

The island stood in the centre of the river, separated from the shore on one side by the channel, through which both boats had already passed, and on the other by a narrow stretch of water which barely covered the bar the *Rover* purposed to cross.

When she pointed for it, the *Wave* promptly gave up chasing her, and made for the channel with the intention of heading her off on the other side of the island in the event of her crossing the bar.

"She's turned back!" exclaimed the captain of the *Rover*. "Now if we can only clear it, we'll have a beautiful start on her. Sit perfectly still, and if you hear her centre-board scrape, pull it up, and trim her to keep her keel level."

Slowly the *Rover* drifted toward the bar; once her centre-board touched, and as the boat moved further into the shallow water the waves rose higher in proportion at the stern.

But her keel did not touch, and as soon as the dark water showed again, her crew gave an exultant shout and pointed her bow toward the Chadwick dock, whence a welcoming cheer came faintly over the mile of water.

"I'll bet they didn't cheer much when we were crossing the bar!" said the younger brother, with a grim chuckle. "I'll bet they thought we were mighty foolish."

"We couldn't have done anything else," returned the superior officer. "It was risky, though. If we'd moved an inch she would have grounded, sure."

"I was scared so stiff that I couldn't have moved if I'd tried to," testified the younger sailor, with cheerful frankness.

Meanwhile the wind had freshened, and white caps began to show over the roughened surface of the river, while sharp, ugly flaws struck the sails of the two contesting boats from all directions, making them bow before the sudden gusts of wind until the water poured over the sides.

But the sharpness of the wind made the racing only more exciting, and such a series of manœuvres as followed, and such a naval battle, was never before seen on the Manasquan River.

The boys handled their boats like veterans, and the boats answered every movement of the rudders and shortening of the sails as a thoroughbred horse obeys its bridle. They ducked and dodged, turned and followed in pursuit, now going free before the wind, now racing, close-hauled, into the teeth of it. Several times a capture seemed inevitable, but a quick turn of the tiller would send the pirates out of danger. And, as many times, the pirate crew almost succeeded in crossing the line, but before they could reach it the revenue cutter would sweep down upon them and frighten them away again.

"We can't keep this up much longer," said the elder Prescott. "There's more water in the boat now than is safe; and every time we go about, we ship three or four bucketfuls more."

As he spoke, a heavy flaw keeled the boat over again, and, before her crew could right her, the water came pouring over the side with the steadiness of a small waterfall. "That settles it for us," exclaimed Prescott, grimly; "we *must* pass the line on this tack, or we sink."

"They're as badly off as we are," returned

his brother. "See how she's wobbling — but she's gaining on us, just the same," he added.

"Keep her to it, then," said the man at the helm. "Hold on to that sheet, no matter how much water she ships."

"If I don't let it out a little, she'll sink!"

"Let her sink, then," growled the chief officer. "I'd rather upset than be caught."

The people on the shore and on the judges' boat appreciated the situation fully as well as the racers. They had seen, for some time, how slowly the boats responded to their rudders and how deeply they were sunk in the water.

All the manœuvring for the past ten minutes had been off the Chadwick dock, and the Atlantic House people, in order to get a better view of the finish, were racing along the bank on foot and in carriages, cheering their champions as they came.

The *Rover* was pointed to cross an imaginary line between the judges' steam-launch and Chadwick's dock. Behind her, not three boat-lengths in the rear, so close that her wash impeded their headway, came the revenue officers, their white caps gone, their hair flying in the wind, and every muscle strained.

Both crews were hanging far over the sides of the boats, while each wave washed the water into the already half-filled cockpits.

"Look out!" shouted the younger Prescott, "here comes another flaw!"

"Don't let that sail out!" shouted back his brother, and as the full force of the flaw struck her, the boat's rail buried itself in the water and her sail swept along the surface of the river.

For an instant it looked as if the boat was swamped, but as the force of the flaw passed over her, she slowly righted again, and with her sail dripping and heavy, and rolling like a log, she plunged forward on her way to the goal.

When the flaw struck the *Wave*, her crew let their sheet go free, saving themselves the inundation of water which had almost swamped the *Rover*, but losing the headway, which the *Rover* had kept.

Before the *Wave* regained it, the pirate craft had increased her lead, though it was only for a moment.

"We can't make it," shouted the younger Prescott, turning his face toward his brother so that the wind might not drown his voice.

"They're almost upon us, and we're settling fast."

"So are they," shouted his brother. "We can't be far from the line now, and as soon as we cross that, it doesn't matter what happens to us!"

As he spoke another heavy gust of wind came sweeping toward them, turning the surface of the river dark blue as it passed over, and flattening out the waves.

"Look at that!" groaned the pirate-king, "we're gone now, surely!" But before the flaw reached them, and almost before the prophetic words were uttered, the cannon on the judges' boat banged forth merrily, and the crowds on the Chadwick dock answered its signal with an unearthly yell of triumph.

"We're across, we're across!" shouted the younger Prescott, jumping up to his knees in the water in the bottom of the boat and letting the wet sheet-rope run freely through his blistered fingers.

But the movement was an unfortunate one.

The flaw struck the boat with her heavy sail dragging in the water, and with young Prescott's weight removed from the rail. She reeled under the gust as a tree bows in

As the two Prescotts scrambled up on the gunwale of their boat, the defeated crew saluted them with cheers.

a storm, bent gracefully before it, and then turned over slowly on her side.

The next instant the *Wave* swept by her, and as the two Prescotts scrambled up on the gunwale of their boat, the defeated crew saluted them with cheers, in response to which the victors bowed as gracefully as their uncertain position would permit.

The new arrival, who had come to Manasquan in the hope of finding something to shoot, stood among the people on the bank and discharged his gun until the barrels were so hot that he had to lay the gun down to cool. And every other man and boy who owned a gun or pistol of any sort, fired it off and yelled at the same time, as if the contents of the gun or pistol had entered his own body. Unfortunately, every boat possessed a tin horn with which the helmsman was wont to signal the keeper of the drawbridge. One evil-minded captain blew a blast of triumph on his horn, and in a minute's time the air was rent with tootings as vicious as those of the steam whistle of a locomotive.

The *Wave* just succeeded in reaching the dock before she settled and sank. A dozen of Chadwick's boarders seized the crew by their coat collars and arms, as they leaped from the sinking boat to the pier, and assisted them to their feet, forgetful in the excitement of the moment that the sailors were already as wet as sponges on their native rocks.

"I suppose I should have stuck to my ship as Prescott did," said the captain of the *Wave* with a smile, pointing to where the judges' boat was towing in the *Rover* with her crew still clinging to her side; "but I'd already thrown you my rope, you know, and there really isn't anything heroic in sticking to a sinking ship when she goes down in two feet of water."

As soon as the Prescotts reached the pier, they pushed their way to their late rivals and shook them heartily by their hands. Then the Atlantic House people carried their crew around on their shoulders, and the two Chadwick's crews were honored in the same embarrassing manner. The proprietor of the Atlantic House invited the entire Chadwick establishment over to a dance and a late supper.

"I prepared it for the victors," he said, "and though these victors don't happen to be the ones I prepared it for, the victors must eat it."

The sun had gone down for over half an hour before the boats and carriages had left the Chadwick dock, and the Chadwick people had an opportunity to rush home to dress. They put on their very best clothes, "just to show the Atlantic people that they *had* something else besides flannels," and danced in the big hall of the Atlantic House until late in the evening.

When the supper was served, the victors were toasted and cheered and presented with a beautiful set of colors, and then Judge Carter made a stirring speech.

He went over the history of the rival houses in a way that pleased everybody, and made all the people at the table feel ashamed of themselves for ever having been rivals at all.

He pointed out in courtly phrases how excellent and varied were the modern features of the Atlantic House, and yet how healthful and satisfying was the old-fashioned simplicity of Chadwick's. He expressed the hope that the two houses would learn to appreciate each other's virtues, and hoped that in the future they would see more of each other.

To which sentiment everybody assented most noisily and enthusiastically, and the proprietor of the Atlantic House said that, in his opinion, Judge Carter's speech was one of the finest he had ever listened to, and he considered that part of it which touched on the excellent attractions of the Atlantic House as simply sublime, and that, with his Honor's permission, he intended to use it in his advertisements and circulars, with **Judge Carter's** name attached.

RICHARD CARR'S BABY.

A few years ago, all the boys living in the town of Princeton who were at that age when it is easy to remember the fall, winter, spring, and summer as the foot-ball, coasting, swimming, and base-ball seasons, regarded Richard Carr as embodying their ideal of human greatness.

When they read in the history primers how George Washington became the Father of his Country, they felt sure that with a like opportunity Richard Carr would come to the front and be the stepfather of his country at least.

They lay in wait for him at the post-office, and as soon as he came in sight, would ask for his mail and run to give it to him; they would go ahead of him on the other side of the street, and cross over and meet him with a very important "How do you do, Mr. Carr?" and were quite satisfied if he gave them an amused "Hello!" in return.

They hung photographs of him and the woodcuts from the daily papers around their rooms, and their efforts to imitate his straight, military walk, with shoulders squared and head erect, were of great benefit to their lungs and personal appearance.

Those ragged hangers-on of the college, too, who picked up odd dimes from the students, by carrying baggage and chasing tennis balls, waited on Richard Carr, and shouted "Hurrah for you, Carr!" whenever that worthy walked by.

Those who have not already guessed the position which Richard Carr held in the college will be surprised to learn that he was captain of the college foot-ball team, and those who cannot understand the admiration that Arthur Waller, and Willie Beck, and the rest of the small fry of Princeton felt for this young man would better stop here — for neither will they understand this story.

Among all these young hero-worshippers, Richard Carr's most devoted follower was Arthur Waller — for, while the other boys, looking upon Carr as their ideal, hoped in time that they might themselves be even as great as he, Arthur felt that to him, this glorious possibility must be denied. Arthur was neither strong nor sturdy, and could, he knew, never hope to be like the captain of the foot-ball team, whose strength and physique seemed, for this reason, all the grander to him.

He never ran after Carr, nor tried to draw his attention as the others did; he was content to watch and form his own ideas about his hero from a distance. Richard Carr was more than the captain of the team to him. He was the one person who, above all others, had that which Arthur lacked — strength; and so Arthur did not merely envy him, — he worshipped him.

Although Arthur Waller was somewhat older in his way of thinking than his friends, he enjoyed the same games they enjoyed, and would have liked to play them, if he had been able; but, as he was not, the boys usually asked him to keep the score, or to referee the matches they played on the cow pasture with one of the college's cast-off foot-balls. On the whole, the boys were very good to Arthur.

It was the first part of the last half of the Yale-Princeton foot-ball match, played on the

Princeton grounds. The modest grand stand was filled with young ladies and college boys, while all the townspeople covered the fences and carriages, and crowded closely on the whitewashed lines, cheering and howling at the twenty-two very dirty, very determined, and very cool young men who ran, rushed, dodged, and "tackled" in the open space before them, — the most interested and least excited individuals on the grounds.

Arthur Waller had crept between the spectators until he had reached the very front of the crowd, and had stood through the first half of the game with bated breath, his finger-nails pressed into his palms, and his eyes following only one of the players. He was entirely too much excited to shout or call as the others did; and he was perfectly silent except for the little gasps of fear he gave involuntarily when Richard Carr struck the ground with more than the usual number of men on top of him.

Suddenly, Mr. Hobbes, of Yale, kicked the ball, but kicked it sideways; and so, instead of going straight down the field, it turned and whirled over the heads of the crowd and settled among the carriages. A panting little Yale man tore wildly after it, beseeching Mr. Hobbes, in agonizing tones, to put him "on side." Mr. Hobbes ran past the spot where the ball would strike, and the Yale man dashed after it through the crowd. Behind him, his hair flying, his eyes fixed on the ball over his head, every muscle on a strain, came Richard Carr. He went at the people blindly, and they tumbled over one another like a flock of sheep, in their efforts to clear the way for him. With his head in the air, he did not see Arthur striving to get out of his way; he only heard a faint cry of pain when he stumbled for an instant, and, looking back, saw the crowd closing around a little boy who was lying very still and white, but who was not crying. Richard Carr stopped as he ran back, and setting Arthur on his feet, asked, "Are you hurt, youngster?" But, as Arthur only stared at him and said nothing, the champion hurried on again into the midst of the fray.

"There is one thing we must have before the next match," said the manager of the team, as the players were gathered in the dressing-rooms after the game, "and that is a rope to keep the people back. They *will* crowd on the field, and get in the way of the half-backs, and, besides, it is not safe for them to stand so near. Carr knocked over a little boy this afternoon, and hurt him quite badly, I believe."

"What's that?" said Richard Carr, turning from the group of substitutes who were explaining how they would have played the game and tendering congratulations.

"I was saying," continued the manager, "that we ought to have a rope to keep the people off the field; they interfere with the game; and they say that you hurt a little fellow when you ran into the crowd during the last half."

"Those boys shouldn't be allowed to stand in front there," said Richard Carr; "but I didn't know I hurt him. Who was he? where does he live? Do you know?"

"It was the widow Waller's son, sir," volunteered Sam, the colored attendant. "That's her house with the trees around it; you can see the roof from here. I think that's where they took him."

"Took him!" exclaimed Richard Carr, catching up his great-coat. "Was he so badly hurt? You wait until I come back, Sam."

A pale, gentle-faced woman, who looked as if she had been crying, came to the door when Richard Carr rang the bell of the cottage which had been pointed out to him from the athletic grounds. When she saw his foot-ball costume, the look of welcome on her face died out very suddenly.

"Does the little boy live here who was hurt on the athletic grounds?" asked Richard Carr, wondering if it could have been the doctor she was expecting.

"Yes, sir," answered the lady, coldly.

"I came to see how he was; I am the man who ran against him. I wish to explain to you how it happened — I suppose you are Mrs. Waller?" (Richard Carr hesitated, and bowed, but the lady only bowed her head in return, and said nothing.) "It was accidental, of course," continued Carr. "He was in the crowd when I ran in after the ball; it was flying over our heads, and I was looking up at it and didn't see him. I hope he is all right now." Before the lady could answer, Richard Carr's eyes wandered from her face and caught sight of a little figure lying on a sofa in the wide hall. Stepping across the floor as lightly as he could in his heavy shoes, Carr sat down beside Arthur on the sofa. "Well, old man," he said, taking Arthur's hands in his, "I hope I didn't hurt you much. No bones broken, — are there? You were very plucky not to cry. It was a very hard fall, and I'm very, very sorry; but I didn't see you, you know."

"Oh, no, sir," said Arthur, quickly, with his eyes fixed on Richard Carr's face. "I knew you didn't see me, and I thought maybe you would come when you heard I was hurt. I don't mind it a bit, from you. Because Willie Beck says — he is the captain of our team, you know — that you wouldn't hurt any one if you could help it; he says you never hit a man on the field unless he's playing foul or trying to hurt some of your team."

Richard Carr doubted whether this recital of his virtues would appeal as strongly to Mrs. Waller as it did to Arthur, so he said, "And who is Willie Beck?"

"Willie Beck! Why, don't you know Willie Beck?" exclaimed Arthur, who was rapidly losing his awe of Richard Carr. "He says he knows you; he is the boy who holds your coat for you during the practice games."

Richard Carr saw he was running a risk of hurting some young admirer's feelings, so he said, "Oh, yes, the boy who holds my coat for me. And he is the captain of your team, is he? Well, the next time you play, you wear this cap and tell Willie Beck and the rest of the boys that I gave it to you because you were so plucky when I knocked you down."

With these words he pressed his orange and black cap into Arthur's hand and rose to go, but Arthur looked so wistfully at him, and then at the captain's cap, that he stopped.

"I'd like to wear it, Mr. Carr," he said slowly. "I'd like to, ever so much, Mamma," he added, turning his eyes to where Mrs. Waller stood looking out at the twilight and weeping softly, — "but you see, sir, I don't play myself. I generally referee. I'm not very strong, sir, not at present; but I will be some day, — won't I, Mamma? And the doctor says I must keep quiet until I am older, and not play games that are rough. For he says if I got a shock or a fall I might not get over it, or it might put me back — and I do so want to get well just as soon as I can. You see, sir, it's my spine——"

Richard Carr gave a sharp gasp of pain and dropped on his knees beside the sofa, and buried his face beside the boy's on the pillow, with his arms thrown tightly around his shoulder.

For a moment Arthur looked at him startled and distressed, and patted Richard Carr's broad back to comfort him; and then he cried:

"Oh, but I didn't mean to blame *you*, Mr. Carr! I know you didn't see me. Don't you worry about me, Mr. Carr. I'm going to get well some day. Indeed I am, sir!"

Whether it was that the surgeon whom Richard Carr's father sent on from New York knew more about Arthur's trouble than the other doctors did, or whether it was that Richard Carr saw that Arthur had many medicines, pleasant and unpleasant, which his mother had been unable to get for him, I do not know, — but I do know that Arthur got better day by day.

And day after day, Richard Carr stopped

on his way to the field, and on his way back again, to see his "Baby," as he called him, and to answer the numerous questions put to him by Arthur's companions. They always assembled at the hour of Richard Carr's arrival in order to share some of the glory that had fallen on their comrade, and to cherish and carry away whatever precious thoughts Richard Carr might let drop concerning football, or the weather, or any other vital topic on which his opinion was decisive.

As soon as the doctor said Arthur could be moved, Richard Carr used to stop for him in a two-seated carriage and drive him in state to the foot-ball field. And after he had drawn up the carriage where Arthur could get a good view of the game, he would hand over the reins to one of those vulture-like individuals who hover around the field of battle, waiting for some one to be hurt, and who are known as "substitutes." In his orange and black uniform, one of these fellows made a very gorgeous coachman indeed.

And though the students might yell, and the townspeople shout ever so loudly, Richard Carr only heard one shrill little voice, which called to him above all the others; and as that voice got stronger day by day, Richard Carr got back his old spirit and interest in the game, which, since the Yale match, he seemed to have lost.

The team said Richard Carr's "Baby" brought them luck, and they called him their "Mascot," and presented him with a flag of the college colors; and when the weather grew colder they used to smother him in their white woollen jerseys, so that he looked like a fat polar bear.

It was a very pretty sight, indeed, to see how Richard Carr and the rest of the team, whenever they had scored or had made a good play, would turn first for their commendation to where Arthur sat perched above the crowd, waving his flag, his cheeks all aglow, and the substitute's arm around him to keep him from falling over in his excitement. And the other teams who came to play at Princeton soon learned about the captain's "Baby," and inquired if he were on the field; and if he was, they would go up and gravely shake hands with him, as with some celebrated individual holding a public reception.

Richard Carr is out West now at the head

of a great sheep ranch, and Arthur Waller enters Princeton next year. I do not know whether he will be on the team, though he is strong enough; but I am sure he will help to hand down the fame of Richard Carr, and that he will do it in such a way that his hero will be remembered as the possessor of certain qualities, perhaps not so highly prized, but almost as excellent, as were those which fitted him to be captain of the team.

THE GREAT TRI-CLUB TENNIS TOURNAMENT.

CHARLES COLERIDGE GRACE, as he was called by the sporting editors, or Charley Grace, as he was known about college, had held the tennis championship of his Alma Mater ever since he had been a freshman.

Even before that eventful year he had carried off so many silver cups and highly ornamented racquets at the different tournaments all over the country, that his entering college was quite as important an event to the college as it was to Charles.

His career was not marked by the winning of any scholarships, nor by any brazen prominence in the way of first honors; and though the president may have wondered at the frequency of his applications to attend funerals, marriages, and the family dentist, he was always careful to look the other way when he met him hurrying to the station with three racquets in one hand and a travelling bag in the other.

Nor was he greatly surprised to read in the next morning's paper that "this brought the winner of the last set and Charles Coleridge Grace together in the finals, which were won by Mr. Grace, 6-4, 6-4, 6-2."

It was near the end of the first term in Grace's junior year, and at the time when the dates of tournaments and examinations were hopelessly clashing, that he received another of many invitations to attend an open tournament. This particular circular announced that the N. L. T. A. of the United States had given the Hilltown Tennis Club permission to hold on their own grounds a tournament for the championship of the State.

Mr. Grace was cordially invited to participate, not only through the formal wording of the circular, but in a note of somewhat extravagant courtesy signed by the club's secretary.

Hilltown is a very pretty place, and some of its people are very wealthy. They see that it has good roads for their village-carts and landaus to roll over, and their Queen Anne cottages are distinctly ornamental to the surrounding landscape.

They have also laid out and inclosed eight tennis-courts of both clay and turf, to suit every one's taste, and have erected a club-house which is apparently fashioned after no one's. Every year Hilltown invited the neighboring tennis-clubs of Malvern and Pineville to compete with them in an inter-club tournament, and offered handsome prizes which were invariably won by representatives of Hilltown.

But this year, owing chiefly to the energies of Mr. C. Percy Clay, the club's enthusiastic secretary, Hilltown had been allowed to hold a tournament on its own tennis-ground for the double and single championship of the State. This honor necessitated the postponement of the annual tri-club meeting until ten days after the championship games had been played.

The team who did the playing for the Hilltown club were two young men locally known as the Slade brothers.

They were not popular, owing to their assuming an air of superiority over every one in the town, from their father down to C.

Percy Clay. But as they had won every prize of which the tennis-club could boast, they of necessity enjoyed a prominence which their personal conduct alone could not have gained for them.

Charles Grace arrived at Hilltown one Wednesday morning. All but the final game of the doubles had been played off on the two days previous, and the singles were to be begun and completed that afternoon. The grounds were well filled when he reached them, and looked as pretty as only pretty tennis-grounds can look when they are gay with well-dressed girls, wonderfully bright blazers, and marquees of vividly brilliant stripes.

Grace found the list of entries to the singles posted up in the club-house, and discovered that they were few in number, and that there was among them only one name that was familiar to him.

As he turned away from the list, two very young and bright-faced boys, in very well-worn flannels, came up the steps of the club-house just as one of the Slades was leaving it.

"Hullo," said Slade, "you back again?"

It was such an unusual and impertinent welcome that Grace paused in some surprise and turned to listen.

The eldest of the boys laughed good-naturedly and said: "Yes, we're here, Mr. Slade. You know we drew a bye, and so we play in the finals."

"Well, of course you'll play my brother and myself then. I hope the novelty of playing in the last round won't paralyze you. If it doesn't, we will," he added with a short laugh. "I say, Ed," he continued, turning to his elder brother, "here are Merton and his partner come all the way from Malvern to play in the finals. They might have saved their car-fare, don't you think?"

The elder brother scowled at the unfortunate representatives of Malvern.

"You don't really mean to make us stand out here in the hot sun fooling with you, do you?" he asked impatiently. "You'll only make a spectacle of yourselves. Why don't you drop out? We've beaten you often enough before, I should think, to suit you, and we want to begin the singles."

But the Malvern youths were not to be browbeaten. They said they knew they would be defeated, but that the people at Malvern were very anxious to have them play, and had insisted on their coming up. "They wish to see what sort of a chance we have for the tri-club tournament, next week," they explained.

"Well, we'll show what sort of chance you have with a vengeance," laughed one of the brothers. "But it really is hard on us."

The two boys flushed, and one of them began hotly, "Let me tell you, Mr. Slade," —but the other put his hand on his arm, saying, "What's the use?" and pushed him gently toward the grounds.

The Slades went into the club-house grumbling.

"Nice lot, those home players," soliloquized Grace. "I'll pound the life out of them for that!"

He was still more inclined to revenge the Malvern youths later, after their defeat by the Slades, — which was not such a bad defeat after all, as they had won one of the four sets, and scored games in the others. But the Slades, with complete disregard for all rules of hospitality to say nothing of the etiquette of tennis, kept up a running comment of ridicule and criticism on their hopeful opponents' play, and, much to Grace's disgust, the spectators laughed and encouraged them. The visitors struggled hard, but everything was against them; they did not understand playing as a team, and though they were quick and sure-eyed enough, and their service was wonderfully strong, the partiality of the crowd "rattled" them, and the ridicule of their opponents was not likely to put them more at their ease.

The man who had been asked to umpire with Grace was a college man, and they both had heard all that went on across the net in the final round. So when their duties were over, they went up to the defeated Malvernites and shook hands with them, and said something kind to them about their playing.

But the cracks did not congratulate the winners. Indeed, they were so disgusted with the whole affair that they refused to be lionized by Mr. Clay and the spectators in any way, but went off to the hotel in the village for luncheon, — which desertion rendered the spread on the grounds as flat as a coming-of-age dinner with the comer-of-age left out.

After luncheon, Thatcher, the other collegian, had the pleasure of defeating the younger Slade in two straight sets, to his own and Grace's satisfaction; but Mr. Thatcher's satisfaction was somewhat dampened when Grace polished him off in the next round, after a game which Grace made as close as he could.

Other rounds were going on in the other courts, and at five o'clock Grace and the elder Slade came together in the finals. Thatcher had gone home after wishing his conqueror luck, and Grace was left alone. He was not pleased to see that Slade's brother was to act as one of the umpires, as he had noticed that his decisions in other games were carelessly incorrect.

But he was in no way prepared for what followed.

For the younger Slade's umpiring in the final game was even more efficient in gaining points for the Hilltown side than was the elder's playing.

It was a matter of principle with Grace, as with all good players, never to question an umpire's decision, and he had been taught the good old rule to "Never kick in a winning game." But the decisions were so outrageous that it soon came too close to being a losing game for him to allow them to continue. So, finally, after a decision of the brother's had given Slade the second one of the two sets, Grace went to the referee and asked that some one be appointed to act in Mr. Slade's place, as he did not seem to understand or to pay proper attention to the game.

"Mr. Slade's decisions have been simply ridiculous," said Grace, "and they have all been against myself. This may be due to ignorance or carelessness, but in any case I object to him as an umpire most emphatically."

"Well, you can object to him all you please," retorted the elder brother. "If you don't like the way this tournament is conducted you can withdraw. You needn't think you can come down here and attempt to run everything to suit yourself, even if you are a crack player. Do you mean to forfeit the game or not?"

"It seems to me, gentlemen," stammered Mr. Percy Clay, excitedly, "that if Mr. Grace desires another umpire —"

"Oh, you keep out of this, will you!"

retorted the omnipotent Slade, and Mr. Clay retreated hurriedly.

Grace walked back into the court, and nodded to the referee that he was ready to go on.

He was too angry to speak, but he mentally determined to beat his opponent so badly, umpire or no umpire, that his friends would avoid tennis as a topic of conversation for months to come.

This incendiary spirit made him hammer the innocent rubber balls to such purpose that the elder Slade was almost afraid of his life, and failed to return more than a dozen of the opponent's strokes in the next two sets.

His brother's decisions were now even more ridiculous than before, but Grace pretended not to notice them.

The game now stood two straight sets in Grace's favor, and one set 6–5 in Slade's — or in favor of both the Slades, for they had both helped to win it.

Grace had four games love, in the final set, when in running back after a returned ball he tripped and fell over an obstacle, spraining his right ankle very badly. The obstacle proved to be the leg of one of the Hilltown youths who was lying in the grass with his feet stuck out so far that they touched the line.

Grace got up and tried to rest his weight on his leg, and then sat down again very promptly.

He shut his teeth and looked around him.

Nobody moved except Mr. Clay, who asked anxiously if Grace were hurt. Grace said that he was; that he had sprained his ankle.

The young gentleman over whom he had fallen had by this time curled his legs up under him, but made no proffer of assistance or apology.

"Oh, that's an old trick!" Grace heard the younger Slade say, in a tone which was meant to reach him. "Some men always sprain their ankles when they are not sure of winning. I guess he'll be able to walk before the year's out."

Grace would have got up then and there and thrashed the younger Slade, ankle or no ankle, if he had not been pounced upon by the two Malvern boys, who pushed their way through the crowd with a pail of lemonade and a half dozen towels that they had picked up in the club-house. They slipped off his shoe and stocking, and dipping a towel in the iced lemonade, bound it about his ankle and repeated the operation several times, much to Grace's relief.

"This lemonade was prepared for drinking purposes, I fancy," said one of them, "but we couldn't find anything else. I never heard of its being good for sprains, but it will have to do. How do you feel now?"

"All right, thank you," said Grace. "I've only these two games to play now, and it's my serve. I needn't run around much in that. Just give me a lift, will you? Thanks."

But as soon as Grace touched his foot to the ground, the boys saw that he was anything but all right. His face grew very white, and his lips lost their color. Whenever he moved he drew in his breath in short, quick gasps, and his teeth were clinched with pain.

He lost his serve, and the next game as well, and before five minutes had passed he was two games to the bad in the last set.

The Malvern boys came to him and told him to rest; that he was not only going to lose the game, but that he might be doing serious injury as well to his ankle, which was already swelling perceptibly. But Grace only unlaced his shoe the further and set his teeth. One of the Malvernites took upon himself to ask the referee if he did not intend giving Mr. Grace a quarter of an hour's "time" at least.

The referee said that the rules did not say anything about sprained ankles.

"Why, I know of tennis matches," returned the Malvernite champion excitedly, "that have been laid over for hours because of a sprained ankle. It will be no glory to Mr. Slade to win from a man who has to hop about on one foot, and no credit either."

"Mr. Grace is a crack player, and I'm not," said Slade; "but I asked no favors of him on that account, and I don't expect him to ask any of me."

"I haven't asked any of you!" roared Grace, now wholly exasperated with anger and pain, "and you'll wait some time before I do. Go on with the game."

The ankle grew worse, but Grace's playing improved, notwithstanding. He felt that he would rather beat "that Slade man" than the champion himself; and he won each of his serves, not one of the balls being returned.

They were now "five all," and the expressed excitement was uproarious in its bitterness and intensity.

Slade had the serve, and it was with a look of perfect self-satisfaction that he pounded the first ball across the net. Grace returned it, and the others that followed brought the score up to 'vantage in Slade's favor, so that he only needed one more point to win.

The people stood up in breathless silence. Grace limped into position and waited, Slade bit his under lip nervously, and served the ball easily, and his opponent sent it back to him like an arrow; it struck within a foot of the serving line on the inside, making the score "deuce."

"Outside! Game and set in favor of Mr. Slade," chanted the younger Slade with an exultant cry.

"What!" shouted Grace and the two Malvernites in chorus.

But the crowd drowned their appeal in exclamations of self-congratulation and triumph.

"Did you see that ball?" demanded Grace of the referee.

"I did," said that young man.

"And do you mean to tell me it was out?"

"It was — I do," stammered the youth. "You heard what Mr. Slade said."

"I don't care what Mr. Slade said. I appeal to you against the most absurd decision ever heard or given on a tennis-field."

"And I support Mr. Slade," replied the referee.

"Oh, very well!" said Grace, with sudden quietness. "Come," he whispered to his two lieutenants, "let's get out of this. They'll take our watches next!" And the three slowly made their way to the club-house.

They helped Grace into his other clothes and packed up his tennis-flannels for him. He was very quiet and seemed more concerned about his ankle than over the loss of the State championship.

Grace and his two supporters were so long in getting to the station, no one having offered Grace a carriage, that he missed his train.

He was very much annoyed, for he was anxious to shake the dust of Hilltown from his feet, and he was more than anxious about his ankle.

"Mr. Grace," said Merton, "Prior and I were wondering if you would think we were presuming on our short acquaintance if we asked you to come home with us to Malvern. You can't get back to college to-night from here, and Malvern is only ten miles off. My father is a doctor and could tell you what you ought to do about your ankle, and we would be very much pleased if you would stay with us."

"Yes, indeed, we would, Mr. Grace," echoed the younger lad.

"Why, it's very kind of you; you're very good indeed!" stammered Grace; "but I am afraid your family are hardly prepared to receive patients at all hours, and to have the house turned into a hospital."

Merton protested with dignity that he had asked Grace as a guest, not as a patient; and they finally compromised upon Grace's consenting to go on to Malvern, but insisting on going to the hotel.

Grace had not been at the Malvern Hotel, which was the only one in the place, and more of an inn than a hotel, for over ten minutes before Dr. Merton arrived in an open carriage and carried him off, whether he would or no, to his own house, where, after the ankle was dressed, Grace was promptly put to bed.

In the morning, much to his surprise, he

found that the swelling had almost entirely disappeared, and he was allowed in consequence to come down to the breakfast-table with the family, where he sat with his foot propped up on a chair. He was considered a very distinguished invalid and found it hard not to pose as a celebrity in the cross-fire of admiring glances from the younger Merton boys and the deferential questions of their equally young sisters.

After breakfast, he was assisted out on to the lawn and placed in a comfortable wicker chair under a tree, where he could read his book or watch the boys play tennis, as he pleased. The tennis was so well worth watching that after regarding it critically for half an hour he suddenly pounded the arm of his chair and called excitedly for the boys to come to him. They ran up in some alarm.

"No, there's nothing wrong," he said. "I have a great idea. I see a way for you to get even with those lads at Hilltown and to revenge me by proxy. All you need is a week's training with better players than yourselves for this tri-club tournament and you'll be as good or better than they are now."

Then the champion explained how the

Malvern team, having no worthy opponents to practise against at home, were not able to improve in their playing; that water would not rise above its own level; and that all they required was competitors who were much better than themselves.

"I can teach you something about team-play that you don't seem to understand," said Grace. "I will write to-day to that college chap, Thatcher, to come down with a good partner and they will give you some fine practice."

The Malvern boys were delighted. They wanted the lessons to begin at once, and as soon as the letter was despatched to Thatcher, Grace had his arm-chair moved up near the net and began his lectures on tennis, two boys from the Malvern club acting as the team's opponents.

Grace began by showing the boys the advantage of working as a team and not as individuals, how to cover both alleys at once, and how to guard both the front and back; he told them where to stand so as not to interfere with each other's play, when to "smash" a ball and when to lift it high in the air, where to place it and when to let it alone. Sometimes one play would be repeated over and over again, and though Grace was a sharp master his team were only too willing to do as he commanded whether they saw the advantage of it or not. When the shadows began to grow long, and the dinner gong sounded, Grace told them they could stop, and said they had already made marked improvement, so they went in radiant with satisfaction and exercise, and delightfully tired.

Practice began promptly the next morning, and continued steadily on to luncheon. At two o'clock Thatcher and another player arrived from the college, which was only a few miles distant from Malvern, and Grace gave them an account of his defeat at Hilltown and of the Slade's treatment of the Malvernites.

"You saw, Thatcher," said Grace, "how they abused and insulted those boys. Well, these same boys have treated me as if I were one of their own family. Dr. and Mrs. Merton have done everything that people could do. It has been really lovely, and I think I can show my appreciation of it by bringing back those cups from that hole in the ground called Hilltown. And I ask you to help me."

The college men entered heartily into Grace's humor, and promised to come down every afternoon and give the boys all the practice they wanted.

Every one belonging to the club had heard what was going on, by this time, and the doctor's big front lawn was crowded with people all the afternoon in consequence.

The improvement in the Malvern boys' playing was so great that every one came up to be introduced, and to congratulate Grace on the work he had done. He held quite a levee in his arm-chair.

Mrs. Merton asked the college men to supper, and had some of the Malvern men and maidens to meet them.

The visitors presumably enjoyed their first day very much, for when they returned the next morning they were accompanied by four more collegians, who showed the keenest interest in the practice games.

These four men belonged to that set that is found in almost every college, whose members always seem to have plenty of time to encourage and aid every institution of Alma

Mater, from the debating societies to the tug-of-war team.

These particular four were always on the field when the teams practised; they bought more tickets than any one else for the Glee Club concerts; and no matter how far the foot-ball team might have to wander to play a match, they could always count on the appearance of the faithful four, clad in great-coats down to their heels, and with enough lung power to drown the cheers of a hundred opponents.

Barnes, Blair, Black, and Buck were their proper names, but they were collectively known as the Four B's, the Old Guard, or the Big Four; and Thatcher had so worked on their feelings that they were now quite ready to champion the Malvern team against their disagreeable opponents.

They made a deep impression on the good townsfolk of Malvern. Different people carried them off to supper, but they all met later at Dr. Merton's and sat out on his wide veranda in the moonlight, singing college songs to a banjo accompaniment which delighted the select few inside the grounds and equally charmed a vast number of the uninvited who hung over the front fence.

The practice games continued day after day, and once or twice the Malvern team succeeded in defeating their instructors, which delighted no one more than the instructors themselves.

Grace was very much pleased. He declared he would rather have his boys defeat the Slades than win the national tournament himself, and at the time he said so, he really believed that he would.

He went around on crutches now, and it was very odd to see him vaulting about the court in his excitement, scolding and approving, and shouting, "Leave that ball alone," "Come up, now," "Go back, play it easy," "Smash it," "Played, indeed, sir," "Well placed."

The tri-club tournament opened on Wednesday, and on Tuesday the Four B's, who had been daily visitors to Malvern, failed to appear, but sent instead two big pasteboard boxes, each holding a blazer, cap, and silk scarf, in blue-and-white stripes, the Malvern club colors, which they offered as their share toward securing the Malvern champions' victory.

On the last practice day, Grace balanced

himself on his crutches and gave the boys the hardest serving they had ever tried to stand up against. All day long he pounded the balls just an inch above the net, and when they were able to return three out of six he threw down his racket and declared himself satisfied. "We may not take the singles," he said, "but it looks as if the doubles were coming our way."

Grace and his boys, much to the disgust of the townspeople, all of whom, from the burgess down to the hostler in the Malvern Hotel, were greatly excited over the coming struggle, requested that no one should accompany them to Hilltown. They said if they took a crowd down there and were beaten it would only make their defeat more conspicuous, and that the presence of so many interested friends might also make the boys nervous. If they won, they could celebrate the victory more decorously at home. But Grace could not keep the people from going as far as the depot to see them off, and they were so heartily cheered as they steamed away that the passengers and even the conductor were much impressed.

The reappearance of Grace on crutches,

and of the Malvern boys in their new clothes caused a decided sensation. They avoided any conversation with the Hilltown people, and allowed Grace to act for them in arranging the preliminaries.

Pineville had sent two teams. Hilltown was satisfied with the "State champions," as they now fondly called the Slades, and these, with Malvern's one team, balanced the games evenly.

The doubles opened with Merton and Prior against the second Pineville team, and the State champions against its first. Grace told his boys not to exert themselves, and to play only just well enough to win. They did as he said, and the second Pineville team were defeated in consequence by so few points that they felt quite pleased with themselves. The Slades had but little trouble with the other Pineville team.

Then the finals came on, and the people of Hilltown crowded up to see the demolition of the Malvernites, against whom they were now more than bitter, owing to Grace's evident interest in their success.

The Hilltown element were so anxious to show their great regard for the champions that they had contributed an extra amount of money toward the purchase of prize cups over and above the fixed sum subscribed by each of the three clubs.

"Get those cups ready for us," said the elder Slade, as the four players took their places. Prior looked as if he was going to answer this taunt, but Grace shook his head at him.

Thatcher, whose late service to the Malvern team was unknown, acted at their request as one of the umpires. Two Hilltown men served as the referee and other umpire. The game opened up in a way that caused a cold chill to run down the backs of the Hilltown contingent. The despised Malvernites were transformed, and Hilltown could not believe its eyes.

"Are these the same boys who were here ten days ago?" asked an excited old gentleman.

"They say they are," replied Mr. Percy Clay, gloomily, "but they don't look it."

The Slades felt a paralyzing numbness coming over them as ball after ball came singing back into their court, placed in odd corners just out of reach of their racquets.

They held a hurried consultation, and rolled up their sleeves a little higher and tossed away their caps.

Grace had a far-away and peaceful look in his eyes that made the crowd feel nervous. The first set went six to four in favor of Malvern. Then the crowd surrounded the champions and poured good advice and reproaches upon them, which did not serve to help either their play or their temper.

The result of the second set convinced the umpire and referee that it was time to take a hand in the game themselves, and the decisions at once became so unfair that Grace hobbled over to that end of the court to see after things. But his presence had no effect on the perceptions of the Hilltown umpire. So he hobbled back to Thatcher and asked him what they had better do about it. Thatcher said he was powerless, and Grace regretted bitterly that he had not brought a crowd with him to see fair play, for the boys were getting rattled at being robbed of so many of their hard-won points. To make matters worse, the crowd took Thatcher in hand, and disputed every decision he gave against Hilltown. Thatcher's blood rose at this, and forgetting that the usual procedure would not be recognized by a Hilltown crowd, he turned on the spectators and told them that he would have the next man who interfered or questioned his decisions expelled from the grounds.

His warning was received with ripples of laughter and ironical cheers.

"Who's going to put us out?" asked the Hilltown youths, derisively. But Thatcher had spoken in a rather loud voice, and his words and the answer to them had reached the ears of four straight-limbed young men who were at that moment making their way across the grounds. They broke into a run when they heard Thatcher's angry voice, and, shoving their way through the big crowd with an abruptness learned only in practice against a rush line on a foot-ball field, stood forth on the court in all the glory of orange and black blazers.

"The Four B's!" exclaimed Grace, with a gasp of relief.

"What seems to be the matter, Thatcher?" asked Black, quietly. "Whom do you want put out?"

"Who are you?" demanded Mr. Clay, running up in much excitement. "Get off this court. You'll be put out yourselves if you attempt to interfere."

Several of the Hilltown young men ran to Mr. Clay's assistance, while one of the Slades leaped over the net and seized Mr. Clay by the shoulder.

"Don't be a fool, Clay!" he whispered. "I know those men. Two of them play on the foot-ball team, and if they felt like it they could turn the whole town out of the grounds. Leave them alone."

Mr. Clay left them alone.

"Go on, Thatcher," said Black, with a nod, "if any of these gentlemen object to any decision, we will discuss it with them. That's what we're here for." Two of the Big Four seated themselves at the feet of the Hilltown umpire, and looked wistfully up at him whenever he made a close decision. It was remarkable how his eyesight was improved by their presence.

The Malvern boys beamed with confidence again. The second set went to them, 6-4. Grace was so delighted that he excitedly stamped his bad foot on the turf, and then howled with pain.

The last set was "for blood," — as one of the four collegians said.

The Slades overcame their first surprise, and settled down to fight for every point. The Malvernites gave them all the fight they wanted. One by one the games fell now on one side, now on the other side of the net. And when it came five games all, the disgust and disappointment of the crowd showed itself in shouts and cheers for their champions and hoots for their young opponents.

But all the cheering and hooting could not change the result.

"Set and game! Malvern wins!" shouted Thatcher, and then, forgetting his late judicial impartiality, threw his arms around Merton's neck and yelled.

The silence of the Hilltown people was so impressive that the wild yell of the college contingent sounded like a whole battery of skyrockets instead of only four, and Grace sat down on the court and pounded the ground with his crutches.

"That's enough for me," he cried; "I don't care for the singles. I know when I've had enough! I'd have two sprained ankles to do it over again!"

Then the Slades announced that the singles would begin immediately after luncheon.

The Malvern contingent went to the hotel to find something to eat, and Blair slipped away to telegraph to Malvern.

Five minutes later the operator at that place jumped as if he had received a shock from his own battery, and ran out into the street shouting, "Malvern's won the doubles, three straight sets!"

Judge Prior's coachman, who was waiting at the station for an express package, turned his horse and galloped back up Malvern's only street, shouting out:

"We've won. Master John and Mr. Merton's won the tennis match."

And then the people set to work to prepare a demonstration.

The Hilltown people thought they had never seen young men so disagreeable as were the Big Four after luncheon. They seated themselves like sentinels at the four corners of the court, and whenever any one ventured to jeer at Malvern's representative they would burst into such an enthusiasm of cheering as to drown the jeers and deafen the spectators.

There was no one in the singles but Slade and Merton, the Pineville representative having decided to drop out. Merton was nervous, and Slade was determined to win. Both played as they had never played before, but Slade's service, which was his strong point, was nothing after the one to which Grace had accustomed Merton. And in spite of Slade's most strenuous efforts the games kept coming slowly and slightly in Merton's favor.

They were two sets all and were beginning the final set, when Barnes arose and disappeared in the crowd. But those of the quartette who were left made noise enough to keep Merton playing his best. It became a more and more bitter fight as the end drew near. Grace was so excited that not even his sprained ankle could keep him quiet, and Thatcher had great difficulty in restraining a desire to shout. At last Merton got "'vantage," with only one point to win, but he missed the next ball and back went the score to "deuce" again. Three times this happened, and three times the college men half rose from the ground expecting to cheer, and then sank back again. "If he does that again," said Grace, "I'll have nervous prostration!" But he didn't do it again. He smashed the next ball back into Slade's court far out of his way, and then pulled down his sleeves as unconcernedly as if he had been playing a practice game.

The next moment Prior and the others had lifted him up on their shoulders, and were tramping around the field with him shouting, "What's the matter with Malvern?" and "We *are* the people!" and many other such highly ridiculous and picturesque cries of victory.

And then there came a shout from the entrance to the grounds, and up the carriage-way rode Barnes mounted on top of an old-fashioned, yellow-bodied stage-coach that he had found in some Hilltown livery-stable and decorated from top to bottom with the Malvern colors. He had four horses in hand, and he was waving his whip and shouting as if a pack of wolves or Indians were in close pursuit.

The boys clambered up on top of the coach and began blowing the horns and affixing the new brooms that Barnes had thoughtfully furnished for them. They were in such a hurry to start that they forgot the prizes;

and if Grace had not reminded the boys, they would have gone home content without the tokens of victory.

The faces of Mr. Percy Clay and the other contributors to the silver cups when they saw the prizes handed up to that "Malvern gang," as they now called them, were most pitiful.

"Fancy our giving two hundred dollars extra for those cups, and then having them go to Malvern!" groaned Mr. Clay.

The boys took the prizes without remark, and had the courtesy not to open the boxes in which the cups reposed on blue velvet until they were out of sight of the men who had lost them with such bad grace.

But when once they were on the road, with the wind whistling around their hats and the trees meeting over their heads and the sun smiling its congratulations as it sank for the night, they examined the cups, and Grace said he had never seen any handsomer.

It really seemed as if the ten miles was covered in as many minutes, and though dogs ran out and barked at them, and the people in the fields stared at them as if they thought they were crazy, and although Barnes insisted on driving over every stone he could find and almost upsetting them, they kept up their spirits and shouted and sang the whole way.

The engineer of the train that had taken them up saw the coach on his return trip bounding through the shady high road where it ran parallel with his track, and told the operator at Malvern that "those boys were coming back on top of a circus band-wagon."

And the people of Malvern were ready to receive them, though they were still ignorant of the second victory. The young people lined the high road for a distance beyond the town, and the boys saw them from afar, seated on the fence-rails and in carts and wagons. The other members of the club saw the stage, also, for one of the boys had been up in a tree on the lookout for the last half hour. And they waved the club colors and all the flags they had been able to get at such short notice; but it was not until three of the Big Four stood up on top of the coach at the risk of breaking their necks, and held up the cups and waved them around their heads until they flashed like mirrors, that the club really cheered. And when they saw that there were THREE cups they set up such a hurrah that the cows in the next field tore madly off in a stampede. That night everybody in town came to Dr. Merton's with the village band and thronged the big lawn; and Merton made a speech in which he spoke very highly of Prior, and of the Big Four who had helped to save the day, and of Thatcher, but most of all of Grace.

Then Grace had to speak leaning on his crutches; and the band played and the college boys sang and everybody handled the prizes and admired them even to the champions' satisfaction.

The next day Grace bade his new friends good by and went back to college, where his absence was attributed to his sprained ankle. He thought of the people of Malvern very often, of the twilight evenings spent on Dr. Merton's lawn listening to the college boys' singing, and talking to the girls of the Malvern Tennis Club, and of the glorious victory of his pupils and the friendliness and kindness of his hosts.

He knew he would never forget them, but he hardly thought they would long remember him.

But, two weeks later, the expressman

brought a big box with a smaller black one inside of it; and within, resting on its blue velvet bed, was a facsimile of the prize-cup of the tri-club tournament. And it was marked, "To Charles Coleridge Grace. From the people of Malvern."

And when Grace exhibits the many prizes he has won, they say that it is this cup which he did *not* win that he handles most tenderly and shows with the greatest pride.

THE JUMP AT COREY'S SLIP.

The jump from Corey's slip was never made but by two of the Brick Dust Gang, and though, as it turned out, they were not sorry they had taken it, they served as a warning to all the others of the gang against trying to emulate their daring.

Corey's slip, as everybody knows, is part of Corey's brick-yard, on the East side, near the Twenty-sixth street wharf, and the Brick Dust Gang are so called because they have a hidden meeting-place among the high piles of bricks which none of the other boys, nor the police, nor even the employees of the brick-yard have been able to find. It is known to exist, though, and the gang meet there to smoke and play the accordion and gamble for cigarette pictures, and to pursue such other sinful and demoralizing practices of East side youth as they elect.

The Brick Dust Gang must not be confounded with the Rag Gang of "The Bay," near Thirty-third street, for, while the Rag Gang are thieves and toughs, the Brick Dust Gang are too young to be very wicked, and their "folks" are too respectable to let them go very far astray. The gang got along very well during the winter months, and the hole in the bricks was filled every afternoon after the public schools had closed, with from a dozen to twenty of them.

Buck Mooney was the leader, and no one disputed his claim, for he was a born leader in some respects, just as was his father, who could throw the votes of the Luke J. Mooney Star Social Club wherever they would do himself and the party the most good. But his son Buck was quick-tempered and stronger than he knew, and he had a way of knocking the younger and less pugilistic members of his crowd around which was injudicious; for by this he hurt his own popularity as well as their heads.

He was no bully though, and there was no one who could lead him in any show of physical prowess recognized and practised by the gang. So all through the winter he was easily the leader, and no one stood against him. His fall came in the spring. The coming of the spring meant more to the Brick Dust Gang than to almost any other crowd along the river front, for their knowledge of the brick-yard and its wharf enabled them to bathe in the river quite hidden from the police at any hour of the day, and this means a great deal to those who have felt the stifling heat of the tenements along the East River.

They bathed and swam and dived from the first of May until the autumn came and gave the water such a sharpness that they left it numbed and with chattering teeth, and they began at five in the morning and kept it up late into the night. They lived in the water, and were rather more at home in it than they were on the streets. The workmen in the brick-yard never interfered with them, because the boys helped them in piling the bricks and in unloading the scows and loading the carts; and the police could never catch them, for the reason that the boys always kept a part of the gang posted as sentinels in the yard.

Mooney and Tommy Grant were easily the best swimmers in the crowd. Tommy was four years younger than the leader, and small and consumptive-looking; but he was absurdly strong for his size, and his body was as hard and muscular as a jockey's. The trouble began between the two at the swimming-match at Harlem for all comers, where they both entered for the one-mile race with a turn. The Harlem boys were not in it from the first, and the two down-town boys led all the others by a hundred yards. "The little fellow," as Tommy was called by the crowds on the shore, was the popular favorite; and the crowd was delighted when he came plunging in ahead, swimming so much under water that only one bare shoulder and revolving arm told where he was.

Buck Mooney, the leader of the gang, was a bad second and a bad loser as well. He swore a great deal when his backers pulled him out of the water, and gave every reason for Tommy's success, except that Tommy could swim faster than he could.

When Tommy appeared around the streets the next day with the big gold medal on his coat, and with the words " Champion of the East River" blazoned on it, Mooney felt worse than ever, and grew so ugly over it that some of the gang soon turned against him, and his hold over them disappeared. Little Tommy took his place without any formal election, and Mooney sulked and said unpleasant things about him behind his back.

They never came to blows, but they both grew to hate each other cordially, — principally through the stories their friends told of each to the other, as friends, true friends, are found to do, in all classes of society. So the breach grew very great and the gang was divided and lost its influence. One faction would refuse to act as sentinel for the other, and each claimed the meeting-place. On the whole, it was very unpleasant, and most unsatisfactory to those who loved peace.

It was evident that something must be done; either the gang must separate into two crowds or reunite again under one leader. It was a foolish, dare-devil young Irish boy that suggested how this last and much-desired result could be accomplished. There was a big derrick at the end of the wharf to lift the buckets of coal from the scows, when the place was used for a coal-yard.

Some of the more daring boys had jumped from the middle bar of this derrick, in emulation of Steve Brodie, whose jump from the Brooklyn Bridge and subsequent elevation to the proprietorship of a saloon had stirred up every boy in the East side. It was a dangerous thing to do, because there was an outer row of posts beyond the slip, and whoever jumped had to jump out far enough to strike the water beyond them. For, if he should not jump far enough —

What the Irish boy proposed was that some one should try to dive — not jump — from the very top of the derrick. The derrick was fifty feet above the water, and the outer line of posts was eight feet from the slip and fifteen feet from the line of the derrick. It looked like just what it was — an impossibility — for any one but the coolest and most practised diver.

"If a lad should do it," objected one of the gang, "and 'ud hit them piles, there'd be no getting at him quick e'cept from the top of the derrick. He'd sink afore any one could get around the piles to him from the slip."

"There'd be no need to hurry," said another, grimly. "He'd keep till the police boat picked him up."

"Well, the morgue's handy," commented another, flippantly, with a nod of his head toward Bellevue Hospital, back of them.

As ill luck would have it, Mooney came up just then, and they told him what they were discussing.

"I'll bet Tommy Grant wouldn't be afeard to try it," said one of the youngest.

That was enough for Mr. Mooney. He said with a sneer that Tommy *would* be afraid, and of course Tommy was told of this at once, and Tommy, after a careful survey of the jump, said it was suicide. And then Mooney called him a coward, and said he'd do it, and he'd show him who was fit to lead the gang.

The elder boys told him not to be a fool, Tommy among the number; but he said they were cry-babies, and told them to keep quiet about it and to meet at the wharf at seven that evening.

The tide was low then, and the piles showed high above the water. At high tide they were covered, and besides there were very few people about at that hour.

At seven o'clock twenty of them gathered at the end of the wharf. They were badly scared and wished they were well out of it, but there was no stopping Mooney. The more they begged him not to do it, the more he laughed at them. He climbed the ladder to the top of the derrick alone, and stripped off every thread but his swimming tights and the scapular around his neck. The big posts rose out of the water in front of the slip — black, slimy-looking, and as pitiless as rocks.

Van Bibber and some of his friends in their steam yacht lying at anchor off the New York Yacht Club's wharf saw the boy mounting the ladder and shouted to the other boys to stop him. The other boys would have liked to do what the gentlemen suggested, but it was too late. But Tommy ran half-way up the ladder, begging his rival to come down. Mooney swore at him to go back, and Tommy hung there half-way up and fearful to do more lest he should rattle the ex-leader of the gang.

The gentlemen on the yacht told two of the crew to jump into the rowboat and pick the young fool up, and the sailors ran to cast off the skiff.

Then they saw Mooney outlined against the dark background of the tenements, as motionless as a marble statue on a high pedestal.

He raised his arms slowly over his head until the finger tips met and interlaced, then he bent his knees and his body swung forward. There was a brief, breathless silence as he dived out and down, and then a yell from the yacht and a gasping cry from the boys, as they saw him throw out his hands wildly to save himself, and saw that he had misjudged the distance and would strike the posts. Some of the youngest boys turned sick and sank whimpering to their knees, and six of the older ones dived like one man into the water to pull him out. He had struck the posts with his arm, had turned, striking them again, and then sank without a cry into the river.

The sailors in the rowboat had just started toward the spot and the club men were cursing them for their slowness. The six boys in the water were shut off from Mooney by the posts, and slipped back after they had tried vainly to climb over them.

"He's killed. He'll be drowned. Ah, he's sunk for good," the boys wailed and cried in chorus.

Young Tommy from his post half-way up the ladder, saw that before the boat could reach his rival, or the boys could get around the piles to him, he would be drowned, and so he ran up the rest of the ladder, poised for just a second, and then took the second and last jump that was ever taken from Corey's slip. He cleared the posts by an inch or two, turned in the water before he had gone half-way into it, and dived to where he saw the white body settling towards the bottom.

The sailors in the rowboat reached him in time to pull him out and carry him to the yacht with the bruised and unconscious body of his rival in his arms. Then the gentlemen sent Mooney over to the hospital, and wanted to make up a purse for Tommy, but he said it was "all right" and "hadn't done nuthin' anyhow." It took several weeks for Mooney's leg and arm to knit, and he limped for months afterward.

The gentlemen on the yacht wanted to compromise by giving Tommy a medal, but he said he'd had enough trouble over the last medal, and asked why they did not give it to Mooney, for he had taken the jump in cold blood; "an' I," said Tommy, "just did it because I was in a hurry to get down."

So Van Bibber and the other yachtsmen

gave Mooney a very fine medal, which told that he was the "Champion Diver of the East River." And now there are two leaders to the gang, though each protests that the other is the only one.

THE VAN BIBBER BASEBALL CLUB.

Young Van Bibber decided that he ought to take some people to the circus. He had long outgrown the age when the circus only pleased, but some of the men had said it was the thing to do just as it was the thing to go incognito to see Carmencita dance; and so he purchased a big box in the very centre of the lowest tier and wrote to Mrs. Dick Wassails that it was at her service and that she could fill it with whom she pleased. He added that he would expect them to take supper with him later.

He owed Mrs. Dick, as everybody called her, a great deal for many social favors, and he thought to make things even in this way; but Mrs. Dick was engaged for that evening, and said she was so sorry and begged to be excused. So young Van Bibber sent off a note to the Gramercys, with whom he wished to become more intimate, and whom he wished to put under an obligation. But they were just going abroad and were in the midst of preparations and they also begged to be excused.

It was getting very near the night now, and Van Bibber ran over in his mind the names of all of those people to whom he owed something or who might some day do something for him. He tried the Van Warps, because they owned a yacht, but they were going to a wedding; and he tried the Van Blunts, on account of their house at Lenox, and found that their great uncle had just died and that they were going to the funeral. Then he asked the men in the club, but the one who gave such good dinners thought it would be too much of a bore; and another, whose sister Van Bibber wanted to know better, said he was afraid he would catch cold, and others, all of whom had been civil to him in one way or another, began to make excuses. So young Van Bibber stood on the steps of the club and kicked viciously at the mat. He decided that his friends were a very poor lot. "One would think I was trying to borrow money from them," soliloquized Van Bibber.

"Where to?" asked the driver of the hansom.

"To the circus," said Van Bibber. It was a long ride, and he had time to make up his mind that he had been foolish in starting out; but as he was already more than half-way there he kept on. He had determined to see that circus himself in solitary state from that box, notwithstanding his irresponsive friends.

But at the entrance to the circus three small boys, in every way representatives of the coming "tough," waylaid him for ten cents to get into the side show — only ten cents, that was all they wanted. They did not aspire to such a pinnacle of happiness as the circus itself. But Young Van Bibber saw a way to use his box and to show his smart friends how somebody, at least, appreciated his invitations.

"Go get three more boys like you," he said; "dirty boys that haven't seen the circus, and I'll take you in."

The three youths looked at him uncertainly for a moment.

"Ah, he's kiddin' us," said one of them, doubtfully.

But there was such an innocent and embarrassed expression on young Van Bibber's face that they concluded he must mean it.

"Besides," said one of them, "don't you'se see he's a priest? He wouldn't tell no lies."

Van Bibber for the first time became conscious of his white lawn tie and his long cape-cloak.

"Priests don't go to circuses," suggested one of the trio.

"Are you going to get those other boys or not?" asked Van Bibber, impatiently. It really seemed as if nobody was willing to go with him. But there was over a dozen boys about him by this time, and he picked out three of the smallest and raggedest. Then he shoved them all into the circus before him like so many chickens and saw, without caring, that the men by the door were laughing at him.

The boys raced about at first and yelled to each other to come see this animal, and to watch that one shaking the bars. Van Bibber wandered around after them. They seemed to be having a very good time, and he felt a queer sensation of satisfaction in some one else's pleasure which was oddly pleasing.

Then they flocked back to him again and informed him it was time to "get into the show part," and so he led them, to the grave disgust of the attendants, to the principal box in the place.

"My eyes! but I wish de boys could see me now," said one of them, pride and happiness beaming from every feature of his face. "I guess this is old man Barnum's box, for sure."

Van Bibber sat in the back of the box. He didn't mind how the people around them smiled. He felt himself very far above them, and in a position to do as many eccentric things as he pleased. And he found himself enjoying the show and the friendly interest his guests took in him, and in their fear lest he couldn't see everything, or that he might miss what the clowns said.

He stopped the man who sold peanuts and candies, and distributed them lavishly. It was cheaper by far than a Delmonico supper, and he enjoyed seeing the half-famished way in which the young rascals fell upon the supplies and stowed them away. They were really very noisy and wildly excited, but he didn't care. He never remembered having given anybody so much extreme pleasure before in his life.

When it was all over and the big spectacular show that had held them breathless had ended, he fought his way out to the waiting hansom, very well pleased with the night's experience. But before he got away his guests crowded around him at the door, and one of them, who, as they had privately informed him, was no less distinguished an individual than the captain of Open Lots Baseball Club, of which they were all members, thanked him very civilly and asked him his name. He gave the captain his card with grave politeness and shook hands with all of them with equal solemnity, and then drove down town and had a solitary supper. On the whole, he concluded that though he had made nothing by it, he had not wasted the box, and he went to bed satisfied.

And two days later he received in a very dirty envelope the following epistle:

DEAR SIR — At a meeting of the Open Lots Baseball Club it was voted, on account of your kindness, to change the name to the Courtland Van Bibber Baseball Club, which it is now, as a mark of our apreshun of your kindness. Truly yours,

TERENCE FAHEY McGLOIN,
Capt. C. Van. B. B. B. C.

"So," said Van Bibber, as he put the letter carefully away, "It pays to go out into the highways, after all."

THE STORY OF A JOCKEY.

Young Charley Chadwick had been brought up on his father's farm in New Jersey. The farm had been his father's before his father died, and was still called Chadwick's Meadows in his memory. It was a very small farm, and for the most part covered with clover and long, rich grass, that were good for pasturing, and nothing else. Charley was too young, and Mrs. Chadwick was too much of a housekeeper and not enough of a farmer's wife, to make the most out of the farm, and so she let the meadows to the manager of the Cloverdale Stock Farm. This farm is only half a mile back from the Monmouth Park race track at Long Branch.

The manager put a number of young colts in it to pasture, and took what grass they did not eat to the farm. Charley used to ride these colts back to the big stables at night, and soon grew to ride very well, and to know a great deal about horses and horse breeding and horse racing. Sometimes they gave him a mount at the stables, and he was permitted to ride one of the race horses around the private track, while the owner took the time from the judges' stand.

There was nothing in his life that he enjoyed like this. He had had very few pleasures, and the excitement and delight of tearing through the air on the back of a great animal, was something he thought must amount to more than anything else in the world. His mother did not approve of his spending his time at the stables, but she found it very hard to refuse him, and he seemed to have a happy faculty of picking up only what was good, and letting what was evil pass by him and leave him unhurt. The good that he picked up was his love for animals, his thoughtfulness for them, and the forbearance and gentleness it taught him to use, with even the higher class of animals who walk on two legs.

He was fond of all the horses, because they were horses; but the one he liked best was Heroine, a big black mare that ran like an express train. He and Heroine were the two greatest friends in the stable. The horse loved him as a horse does love its master sometimes, and though Charley was not her owner, he was in reality her master, for Heroine would have left her stall and carried Charley off to the ends of the continent if he had asked her to run away.

When a man named Oscar Behren bought Heroine, Charley thought he would never be contented again. He cried about it all along the country road from the stables to his home, and cried about it again that night in bed. He knew Heroine would feel just as badly about it as he did, if she could know they were to be separated. Heroine went off to run in the races for which her new master had entered her, and Charley heard of her only through the newspapers. She won often, and became a great favorite, and Charley was afraid she would forget the master of her earlier days before she became so famous. And when he found that Heroine was entered to run at the Monmouth Park race track, he became as excited over the prospect of seeing his old friend again, as though he were going to meet his promised bride, or a long-lost brother who had accumulated several millions in South America.

He was at the station to meet the Behren horses, and Heroine knew him at once and he knew Heroine, although she was all blanketed up and had grown so much more beautiful to look at, that it seemed like a second and improved edition of the horse he had known. Heroine won several races at Long Branch, and though her owner was an unpopular one, and one of whom many queer stories were told, still Heroine was always ridden to win, and win she generally did.

The race for the July Stakes was the big race of the meeting, and Heroine was the favorite. Behren was known to be backing her with thousands of dollars, and it was almost impossible to get anything but even money on her. The day before the race McCallen, the jockey who was to ride her, was taken ill, and Behren was in great anxiety and greatly disturbed as to where he could get a good substitute. Several people told him it made no difference, for the mare was as sure as sure could be, no matter who rode her. Then some one told him of Charley, who had taken out a license when the racing season began, and who had ridden a few unimportant mounts.

Behren looked for Charley and told him he would want him to ride for the July Stakes, and Charley went home to tell his mother about it, in a state of wild delight. To ride the favorite, and that favorite in such a great race, was as much to him as to own and steer the winning yacht in the trans-atlantic match for the cup.

He told Heroine all about it, and Heroine seemed very well pleased. But while he was standing hidden in Heroine's box stall, he heard something outside that made him wonder. It was Behren's voice, and he said in a low tone: —

"Oh, McCallen's well enough, but I didn't want him for this race. He knows too much. The lad I've got now, this country boy, wouldn't know if the mare had the blind staggers."

Charley thought over this a great deal, and all that he had learned on the tracks and around the stables came to assist him in judging what it was that Behren meant; and that afternoon he found out.

The race track with the great green enclossures and the grand stand as high as a hill, were as empty as a college campus in vacation time, but for a few of the stable boys and some of the owners, and a colored waiter or two. It was interesting to think what it would be like a few hours later when the trains had arrived from New York with eleven cars each and the passengers hanging from the steps, and the carriages stretched all the way from Long Branch. Then there would not be a vacant seat on the grand stand or a blade of grass untrampled.

Charley was not nervous when he thought of this, but he was very much excited. Howland S. Maitland, who owned a stable of horses and a great many other expensive things, and who was one of those gentlemen who make the racing of horses possible, and Curtis, the secretary of the meeting, came walking towards Charley looking in at the different horses in the stalls.

"Heroine," said Mr. Maitland, as he read the name over the door. "Can we have a look at her?" he said.

Charley got up and took off his hat.

"I am sorry, Mr. Maitland," he said, "but my orders from Mr. Behren are not to allow any one inside. I am sure if Mr. Behren were here he would be very glad to show you the horse; but you see, I'm responsible, sir, and —"

"Oh, that's all right!" said Mr. Maitland pleasantly, as he moved on.

"There's Mr. Behren now," Charley called after him, as Behren turned the corner. "I'll run and ask him."

"No, no, thank you," said Mr. Maitland hurriedly, and Charley heard him add to Mr. Curtis, "I don't want to know the man." It hurt Charley to find that the owner of Heroine and the man for whom he was to ride was held in such bad repute that a gentleman like Mr. Maitland would not know him, and he tried to console himself by thinking that it was better he rode Heroine than some less conscientious jockey whom Behren might order to play tricks with the horse and the public. Mr. Behren came up with a friend, a red-faced man with a white derby hat. He pointed at Charley with his cane. "My new jockey," he said. "How's the mare?" he asked.

"Very fit, sir," Charley answered.

"Had her feed yet?"

"No," Charley said.

The feed was in a trough which the stable

boy had lifted outside into the sun. They were mixing it under Charley's supervision, for as a rider he did not stoop to such menial work as carrying the water and feed; but he always overlooked the others when they did it. Behren scooped up a handful and examined it carefully.

"It's not as fresh as it ought to be for the price they ask," he said to the friend with him. Then he threw the handful of feed back into the trough and ran his hand through it again, rubbing it between his thumb and fingers and tasting it critically. Then they passed on up the row.

Charley sat down again on an overturned bucket and looked at the feed trough, then he said to the stable boys, "You fellows can go now and get something to eat if you want to." They did not wait to be urged. Charley carried the trough inside the stable and took up a handful of the feed and looked and sniffed at it. It was fresh from his own barn; he had brought it over himself in a cart that morning. Then he tasted it with the end of his tongue and his face changed. He glanced around him quickly to see if any one had noticed, and then, with the feed still clenched in his hand, ran out and looked anxiously up and down the length of the stable. Mr. Maitland and Curtis were returning from the other end of the road.

"Can I speak to you a moment, sir?" said Charley anxiously; "will you come in here just a minute? It's most important, sir. I have something to show you."

The two men looked at the boy curiously, and halted in front of the door. Charley added nothing further to what he had said, but spread a newspaper over the floor of the stable and turned the feed trough over on it. Then he stood up over the pile and said, "Would you both please taste that?"

There was something in his manner which made questions unnecessary. The two gentlemen did as he asked. Then Mr. Curtis looked into Mr. Maitland's face, which was full of doubt and perplexity, with one of angry suspicion.

"Cooked," he said.

"It does taste strangely," commented the horse owner gravely.

"Look at it; you can see if you look close enough," urged Curtis excitedly. "Do you see that green powder on my finger? Do you know what that is? An ounce of that would turn a horse's stomach as dry as a lime-kiln. Where did you get this feed?" he demanded of Charley.

"Out of our barn," said the boy. "And no one has touched it except myself, the stable boys, and the owner."

"Who are the stable boys?" demanded Mr. Curtis.

"Who's the owner?" asked Charley.

"Do you know what you are saying?" warned Mr. Maitland sharply. "You had better be careful."

"Careful!" said Charley indignantly. "I will be careful enough."

He went over to Heroine, and threw his arm up over her neck. He was terribly excited and trembling all over. The mare turned her head towards him and rubbed her nose against his face.

"That's all right," said Charley. "Don't you be afraid. I'll take care of *you*."

The two men were whispering together.

"I don't know anything about you," said Mr. Maitland to Charley. "I don't know what your idea was in dragging me into this. I'm sure I wish I was out of it. But this I do know, if Heroine isn't herself to-day, and doesn't run as she has run before, and I say it though my own horses are in against her, I'll have you and your owner before the Racing Board, and you'll lose your license and be ruled off every track in the country."

"One of us will," said Charley stubbornly. "All I want you to do, Mr. Maitland, is to put some of that stuff in your pocket. If anything is wrong they will believe what you say, when they wouldn't listen to me. That's why I called you in. I haven't charged any one with anything. I only asked you and Mr. Curtis to taste the feed that this horse was to have eaten. That's all. And I'm not afraid of the Racing Board, either, if the men on it are honest."

Mr. Curtis took some letters out of his pocket and filled the envelopes with the feed, and then put them back in his pocket, and Charley gathered up the feed in a bucket and emptied it out of the window at the back of the stable.

"I think Behren should be told of this," said Mr. Maitland.

Charley laughed; he was still excited and angry. "You had better find out which way

Mr. Behren is betting, first," he said,—"if you can."

"Don't mind the boy. Come away," said Mr. Curtis. "We must look into this."

The Fourth of July holiday makers had begun to arrive; and there were thousands of them, and they had a great deal of money, and they wanted to bet it all on Heroine. Everybody wanted to bet on Heroine; and the men in the betting ring obliged them. But there were three men from Boston who were betting on the field against the favorite. They distributed their bets in small sums of money among a great many different bookmakers; even the oldest of the racing men did not know them. But Mr. Behren seemed to know them. He met one of them openly, in front of the grand stand, and the stranger from Boston asked politely if he could trouble him for a light. Mr. Behren handed him his cigar, and while the man puffed at it he said: —

"We've got $50,000 of it up. It's too much to risk on that powder. Something might go wrong; you mightn't have mixed it properly, or there mayn't be enough. I've known it miss before this. Minerva she won once with an ounce of it inside her. You'd better fix that jockey."

Mr. Behren's face was troubled, and he puffed quickly at his cigar as the man walked away. Then he turned and moved slowly towards the stables. A gentleman with a field-glass across his shoulder stopped him and asked, "How's Heroine?" and Mr. Behren answered, "Never better; I've $10,000 on her," and passed on with a confident smile. Charley saw Mr. Behren coming, and bit his lip and tried to make his face look less conscious. He was not used to deception. He felt much more like plunging a pitchfork into Mr. Behren's legs; but he restrained that impulse, and chewed gravely on a straw. Mr. Behren looked carefully around the stable, and wiped the perspiration from his fat red face. The day was warm, and he was excited.

"Well, my boy," he said in a friendly, familiar tone as he seated himself, "it's almost time. I hope you are not rattled." Charley said "No," he felt confident enough.

"It would be a big surprise if she went back on us, wouldn't it?" suggested the owner gloomily.

"It would, indeed," said Charley.

"Still," said Mr. Behren, "such things have been. Racin' is full of surprises, and horses are full of tricks. I've known a horse, now, get pocketed behind two or three others and never show to the front at all. Though she was the best of the field, too. And I've known horses go wild and jump over the rail and run away with the jock, and, sometimes, they fall. And sometimes I've had a jockey pull a horse on me and make me drop every cent I had up. You wouldn't do that, would you?" he asked. He looked up at Charley with a smile that might mean anything. Charley looked at the floor and shrugged his shoulders.

"I ride to orders, I do," he said. "I guess the owner knows his own business best. When I ride for a man and take his money I believe he should have his say. Some jockeys ride to win. I ride according to orders." He did not look up after this, and he felt thankful that Heroine could not understand the language of human beings. Mr. Behren's face rippled with smiles. This was a jockey after his own heart. "If Heroine should lose," he said, — "I say, if she should, for no one knows what might happen, — I'd have to abuse you fearful right before all the people. I'd swear at you and say you lost me all my money, and that you should never ride for me again. And they might suspend you for a month or two, which would be very hard on you," he added reflectively. "But then," he said more cheerfully, "if you had a little money to live on while you were suspended it wouldn't be so hard, would it?" He took a large roll of bank bills from his pocket and counted them, smoothing them out on his fat knee and smiling up at the boy.

"It wouldn't be so bad, would it?" he repeated. Then he counted aloud, "Eight hundred, nine hundred, one thousand." He rose and placed the bills under a loose plank of the floor, and stamped it down on them. "I guess we understand each other, eh?" he said.

"I guess we do," said Charley.

"I'll have to swear at you, you know," said Behren, smiling.

"I can stand that," Charley answered.

* * * * *

As the horses paraded past for the July Stakes, the people rushed forward down the

He took a large roll of bank bills from his pocket and counted them.

inclined enclosure and crushed against the rail and cheered whichever horse they best fancied.

"Say, you," called one of the crowd to Charley, "you want to win, you do. I've got $5 on that horse you're a-riding." Charley ran his eyes over the crowd that were applauding and cheering him and Heroine, and calculated coolly that if every one had only $5 on Heroine there would be at least $100,000 on the horse in all.

The man from Boston stepped up beside Mr. Behren as he sat on his dog-cart alone.

"The mare looks very fit," he said anxiously. "Her eyes are like diamonds. I don't believe that stuff affected her at all."

"It's all right," whispered Behren calmly. "I've fixed the boy." The man dropped back off the wheel of the cart with a sigh of relief, and disappeared in the crowd. Mr. Maitland and Mr. Curtis sat together on the top of the former's coach. Mr. Curtis had his hand over the packages of feed in his pockets. "If the mare don't win," he said, "there will be the worst scandal this track has ever known." The perspiration was rolling down his face. "It will be the death of honest racing."

"I cannot understand it," said Mr. Maitland. "The boy seemed honest, too."

The horses got off together. There were eleven of them. Heroine was amongst the last, but no one minded that because the race was a long one. And within three-quarters of a mile of home Heroine began to shake off the others and came up slowly through the crowd, and her thousands of admirers yelled. And then Maitland's Good Morning and Reilly swerved in front of her, or else Heroine fell behind them, it was hard to tell which, and Lady Betty closed in on her from the right. Her jockey seemed to be trying his best to get her out of the triangular pocket into which she had run. The great crowd simultaneously gave an anxious questioning gasp. Then two more horses pushed to the front, closing the favorite in and shutting her off altogether.

"The horse is pocketed," cried Mr. Curtis, "and not one man out of a thousand would know that it was done on purpose."

"Wait!" said Mr. Maitland.

"Bless that boy!" murmured Behren, trying his best to look anxious. "She can never pull out of that." They were within half a mile of home. The crowd was panic-stricken and jumping up and down. "Heroine!" they cried, as wildly as though they were calling for help, or the police — "Heroine!"

Charley heard them above the noise of the pounding hoofs, and smiled in spite of the mud and dirt that the great horses in front flung in his face and eyes.

"Heroine," he said, "I think we've scared that crowd about long enough. Now, punish Behren." He sank his spurs into the horse's sides and jerked her head towards a little opening between Lady Betty and Chubb. Heroine sprang at it like a tiger and came neck to neck with the leader. And then, as she saw the wide track empty before her, and no longer felt the hard backward pull on her mouth, she tossed her head with a snort, and flew down the stretch like an express, with her jockey whispering fiercely in her ear.

Heroine won with a grand rush, by three lengths, but Charley's face was filled with anxiety as he tossed up his arm in front of the judges' stand. He was covered with mud and perspiration, and panting with exertion and excitement. He distinguished Mr. Curtis' face in the middle of the wild crowd around him, that patted his legs and hugged and kissed Heroine's head, and danced up and down in the ecstasy of delight.

"Mr. Curtis," he cried, raising his voice above the tumult of the crowd, and forgetting, or not caring, that they could hear, "send some one to the stable, quick. There's a thousand dollars there Behren offered me to pull the horse. It's under a plank near the back door. Get it before he does. That's evidence the Racing Board can't—"

But before he could finish, or before Mr. Curtis could push his way towards him, a dozen stable boys and betting men had sprung away with a yell towards the stable, and the mob dashed after them. It gathered in volume as a landslide does when it goes down hill; and the people in the grand stand and on the coaches stood up and asked what was the matter; and some cried "Stop thief!" and others cried "Fight!" and others said that a bookmaker had given big odds against Heroine, and was "doing a welsh." The mob swept around the corner of the long line of stables like a charge of cavalry, and dashed at Heroine's lodgings. The door was open, and on his knees at the other end was

Behren, digging at the planks with his fingernails. He had seen that the boy had intentionally deceived him; and his first thought, even before that of his great losses, was to get possession of the thousand dollars that might be used against him. He turned his fat face, now white with terror, over his shoulder, as the crowd rushed into the stable, and tried to rise from his knees; but before he could get up, the first man struck him between the eyes, and others fell on him, pummelling him and kicking him and beating him down. If they had lost their money, instead of having won, they could not have handled him more brutally. Two policemen and a couple of men with pitchforks drove them back; and one of the officers lifted up the plank, and counted the thousand dollars before the crowd.

Either Mr. Maitland felt badly at having doubted Charley, or else he admired his riding; for he bought Heroine when Behren was ruled off the race tracks and had to sell his horses, and Charley became his head jockey. And just as soon as Heroine began to lose, Mr. Maitland refused to have her suffer such a degradation, and said she should stop while she could still win. And then he presented her to Charley, who had won so much and so often with her; and Charley gave up his license and went back to the farm to take care of his mother, and Heroine played all day in the clover fields.

Typography by J. S. Cushing & Co., Boston.
Presswork by Berwick & Smith, Boston.

✣ ✣ Charles Scribner's Sons' New and Standard Books for Young Readers for 1895=96 ✣ ✣ ✣ ✣ ✣

A NEW BOOK BY MRS. BURNETT
TWO LITTLE PILGRIMS' PROGRESS

A STORY OF THE CITY BEAUTIFUL. By Mrs. FRANCES HODGSON BURNETT. Illustrated by REGINALD B. BIRCH. Uniform with "Fauntleroy," etc. Square 8vo, $1.50.

The largest and most notable children's book that Mrs. Burnett has written since "Fauntleroy." It is a charming story of a little boy and girl, who, taking their small savings, leave home to visit the World's Fair. This is their Pilgrims' Progress; and their interesting adventures and the happy ending of it all Mrs. Burnett tells as no one else can. It is in the author's best vein and will take place in the hearts of her readers close beside "Fauntleroy."

MRS. BURNETT'S FIVE FAMOUS JUVENILES

LITTLE LORD FAUNTLEROY. Beautifully illustrated by REGINALD B. BIRCH. Square 8vo, $2.00.

"In 'Little Lord Fauntleroy' we gain another charming child to add to our gallery of juvenile heroes and heroines; one who teaches a great lesson with such truth and sweetness that we part from him with real regret."—LOUISA M. ALCOTT.

SARA CREWE; OR, WHAT HAPPENED AT MISS MINCHIN'S. Richly and fully illustrated by REGINALD B. BIRCH. Square 8vo, $1.00.

"It is a story to linger over in the reading, it is so brightly, frankly, sweetly, and tenderly written, and to remember and return to. In creating her little gentlewoman, 'Sara Crewe,' so fresh, so simple, so natural, so genuine, and so indomitable, Mrs. Burnett has added another child to English fiction."—R. H. STODDARD.

LITTLE SAINT ELIZABETH, AND OTHER STORIES. With 12 full-page drawings by REGINALD B. BIRCH. Square 8vo, $1.50.

"Four stories different in kind, but alike in grace and spirit."—SUSAN COOLIDGE.

GIOVANNI AND THE OTHER: CHILDREN WHO HAVE MADE STORIES. With 9 full-page illustrations by REGINALD B. BIRCH. Square 8vo, $1.50.

"Stories beautiful in tone, and style, and color."—KATE DOUGLAS WIGGIN.

PICCINO, AND OTHER CHILD STORIES. Fully illustrated by REGINALD B. BIRCH. Square 8vo, $1.50.

"The history of Piccino's 'two days' is as delicate as one of the anemones that spring in the rock walls facing Piccino's Mediterranean. . . . The other stories in the book have the charm of their predecessor in material and matter. . . . "—Mrs. BURTON HARRISON.

BOOKS BY HOWARD PYLE

A NEW BOOK JUST PUBLISHED

BEHIND THE GARDEN OF THE MOON. A REAL STORY OF THE MOON ANGEL. Written and illustrated by HOWARD PYLE. Square 12mo, $2.00.

Underneath the charm of this original and delightful fairy tale of Mr. Pyle's is a mystical moral significance which gives it the dignity of true literature in addition to its interest of adventure. Out of the truth that great deeds are achieved and high character moulded by entire spiritual consecration, rather than by direct and interested effort, the author has evolved a winning and delightful piece of fanciful fiction, and has illustrated it copiously in his happiest and most characteristically poetical vein.

THE MERRY ADVENTURES OF ROBIN HOOD OF GREAT RENOWN IN NOTTINGHAMSHIRE. With many illustrations. Royal 8vo, $3.00.

"This superb book is unquestionably the most original and elaborate ever produced by any American artist. Mr. Pyle has told, with pencil and pen, the complete and consecutive story of Robin Hood and his merry men in their haunts in Sherwood Forest, gathered from the old ballads and legends. Mr. Pyle's admirable illustrations are strewn profusely through the book."—*Boston Transcript.*

OTTO OF THE SILVER HAND. With many illustrations. Royal 8vo, half leather, $2.00.

"The scene of the story is mediæval Germany in the time of the feuds and robber barons and romance. The kidnapping of Otto, his adventures among rough soldiers, and his daring rescue, make up a spirited and thrilling story. The drawings are in keeping with the text, and in mechanical and artistic qualities as well as in literary execution the book must be greeted as one of the very best juveniles of the year, quite worthy to succeed to the remarkable popularity of Mr. Pyle's 'Robin Hood.'"—*Christian Union.*

THE BUTTERFLY HUNTERS IN THE CARIBBEES

By Dr. EUGENE MURRAY-AARON. With 8 full-page illustrations. Square 12mo, $2.00.

"Our author only reproduces the incidents and scenes of his own life, as an exploring naturalist, in a way to capture the attention of younger readers. The incidents are told entertainingly, and his descriptions of country and the methods of capture of butterflies and bugs of rare varieties are full of interest."
—*Chicago Inter-Ocean.*

A NEW MEXICO DAVID

AND OTHER STORIES AND SKETCHES OF THE SOUTH-WEST. By CHARLES F. LUMMIS. Illustrated. 12mo, $1.25.

"Mr. Lummis has lived for years in the land of the Pueblos; has traversed it in every direction, both on foot and on horseback; and it is an enthralling treat set before youthful readers by him in this series of lively chronicles."—*Boston Beacon.*

STORIES FOR BOYS

By RICHARD HARDING DAVIS. With 6 full-page illustrations. 12mo, $1.00.

"It will be astonishing indeed if youths of all ages are not fascinated with these 'Stories for Boys.' Mr. Davis knows infallibly what will interest his young readers."—*Boston Beacon.*

THE KANTER GIRLS

By MARY L. B. BRANCH. Illustrated by HELEN M. ARMSTRONG. Square 12mo, $1.50.

The adventures of Jane and Prue, two small sisters, among different peoples of the imaginative world—dryads, snow-children, Kobolds, etc.—aided by their invisible rings, their magic boat, and their wonderful birds, are described by the author with great naturalness and a true gift for story-telling. The numerous illustrations are very attractive, and in thorough sympathy with the text.

THE WAGNER STORY BOOK

FIRELIGHT TALES OF THE GREAT MUSIC DRAMAS. By WILLIAM HENRY FROST. Illustrated by SIDNEY R. BURLEIGH. 12mo, $1.50.

"A successful attempt to make the romantic themes of the music dramas intelligible to young readers. The author has full command of his subject, and the style is easy, graceful, and simple."—*Boston Beacon.*

ROBERT GRANT'S TWO BOOKS FOR BOYS

JACK HALL; OR, THE SCHOOL DAYS OF AN AMERICAN BOY. Illustrated by F. G. ATTWOOD. 12mo, $1.25.

"A better book for boys has never been written. It is pure, clean, and healthy, and has throughout a vigorous action that holds the reader breathlessly."
—*Boston Herald.*

JACK IN THE BUSH; OR, A SUMMER ON A SALMON RIVER. Illustrated by F. T. MERRILL. 12mo, $1.25.

"A clever book for boys. It is the story of the camp life of a lot of boys, and is destined to please every boy reader. It is attractively illustrated."
—*Detroit Free Press.*

CZAR AND SULTAN

THE ADVENTURES OF A BRITISH LAD IN THE RUSSO-TURKISH WAR OF 1877-78. By ARCHIBALD FORBES. Illustrated. 12mo, $2.00.

"Very fascinating and graphic. Mr. Forbes is a forcible writer, and the present work has the vigor and intensity associated with his name. It is sure to be popular with youthful readers."—*Boston Beacon.*

JOSEPH THE DREAMER

By the author of "Jesus the Carpenter." 12mo. *In Press.*

The story of Joseph, told in the same popular, interesting, and realistic manner as that of Jesus in the author's former book; not only setting forth truthfully and graphically the life of Joseph, but picturing as well the marvelous state of Egypt in which he lived.

JESUS THE CARPENTER

By A. LAYMAN. 12mo, $1.50.

"I think the idea of this book—the aim and the intention—excellent and the execution beautiful."—Prof. A. B. BRUCE.

A NEW BOOK BY KIRK MUNROE
AT WAR WITH PONTIAC

OR, THE TOTEM OF THE BEAR. A Tale of Redcoat and Redskin. By KIRK MUNROE. With 8 full-page illustrations by J. FINNEMORE. 12mo, $1.25.

A story of old days in America when Detroit was a frontier town and the shores of Lake Erie were held by hostile Indians under Pontiac. The hero, Donald Hester, goes in search of his sister Edith, who has been captured by the Indians. Strange and terrible are his experiences: for he is wounded, taken prisoner, condemned to be burned, and contrives to escape. In the end there is peace between Pontiac and the English, and all things terminate happily for the hero. One dares not skip a page of this enthralling story.

THE WHITE CONQUEROR

A TALE OF TOLTEC AND AZTEC. By KIRK MUNROE. With 8 full-page illustrations by W. S. STACEY. 12mo, $1.25.

"The story is replete with scenes of vivid power; it is full of action and rapid movement; and he must be deficient in receptive faculty who fails to gain valuable historical instruction, along with the pleasure of reading a tale graphically told."
—*Philadelphia Bulletin.*

STORIES OF LITERATURE, SCIENCE, AND HISTORY
By HENRIETTA CHRISTIAN WRIGHT.

A NEW VOLUME JUST ISSUED.

CHILDREN'S STORIES IN AMERICAN LITERATURE, 1660-1860. 12mo, $1.25.
Miss Wright here continues her attractive presentation of literary history begun in her "Children's Stories in English Literature." Elliot, the translator of the Bible into the English language, Irving, Cooper, Prescott, Holmes, Longfellow, Hawthorne, Mrs. Stowe, Whittier, Poe, and Emerson are here considered, bringing the history of the subject down to the period of the Civil War, and treated with constant reference to that side of their works and personalities which most nearly appeals to children.

CHILDREN'S STORIES IN ENGLISH LITERATURE. Two volumes: TALIESIN TO SHAKESPEARE, SHAKESPEARE TO TENNYSON. 12mo, each, $1.25.
"It is indeed a vivid history of the people as well as a story of their literature; and, brief as it is, the author has so deftly seized on all the salient points, that the child who has read this book will be more thoroughly acquainted than many a student of history with the life and thought of the centuries over which the work reaches."—*The Evangelist.*

CHILDREN'S STORIES OF THE GREAT SCIENTISTS. With portraits. 12mo, $1.25.
"The author has succeeded in making her pen-pictures of the great scientists as graphic as the excellent portraits that illustrate the work. Around each name she has picturesquely grouped the essential features of scientific achievement."
—*Brooklyn Times.*

CHILDREN'S STORIES OF AMERICAN PROGRESS. Illustrated. 12mo, $1.25.
"Miss Wright is favorably known by her volume of well-told 'Stories in American History'; and her 'Stories of American Progress' is equally worthy of commendation. Taken together they present a series of pictures of great graphic interest. The illustrations are excellent."—*The Nation.*

CHILDREN'S STORIES IN AMERICAN HISTORY. Illustrated. 12mo, $1.25.
"A most delightful and instructive collection of historical events, told in a simple and pleasant manner. Almost every occurrence in the gradual development of our country is woven into an attractive story for young people."
—*San Francisco Evening Post.*

G. A. HENTY'S POPULAR STORIES FOR BOYS

New Volumes for 1895-96. Each, crown 8vo, handsomely illustrated, $1.50.

Mr. Henty, the most popular writer of Books of Adventure in England, adds three new volumes to his list this fall—books that will delight thousands of boys on this side who have become his ardent admirers.

"Mr. Henty's books never fail to interest boy readers. Among writers of stories of adventure he stands in the very first rank."—*Academy*, London.

"No country nor epoch of history is there which Mr. Henty does not know, and what is really remarkable is that he always writes well and interestingly. Boys like stirring adventures, and Mr. Henty is a master of this method of composition."—*New York Times*.

A KNIGHT OF THE WHITE CROSS

A TALE OF THE SIEGE OF RHODES. With 12 full-page illustrations.

Gervaise Tresham, the hero of this story, joins the Order of the Knights of St. John, and leaving England he proceeds to the stronghold of Rhodes, and becomes a page in the household of the Grand Master. Subsequently, Gervaise is made a Knight of the Grand Cross for valor, while soon after he is appointed commander of a war-galley, and in his first voyage destroys a fleet of Moorish corsairs. During one of his cruises the young knight is attacked on shore, captured after a desperate struggle, and sold into slavery in Tripoli. He succeeds in escaping, however, and returns to Rhodes in time to take part in the splendid defence of that fortress. Altogether a fine chivalrous tale, of varied interest and full noble daring.

THE TIGER OF MYSORE

A STORY OF THE WAR WITH TIPPOO SAIB. With 12 full-page illustrations.

Dick Holland, whose father is supposed to be a captive of Tippoo Saib, goes to India to help him to escape. He joins the army under Lord Cornwallis, and takes part in the campaign against Tippoo. Afterwards he assumes a disguise; enters Seringapatum, the capital of Mysore, rescues Tippoo's harem from a tiger, and is appointed to high office by the tyrant. In this capacity Dick visits the hill fortresses, still in search of his father, and at last he discovers him in the great stronghold of Savandroog. The hazardous rescue which Dick attempts, and the perilous night ride through the enemy's country are at length accomplished, and the young fellow's dangerous mission is done.

THROUGH RUSSIAN SNOWS

A STORY OF NAPOLEON'S RETREAT FROM MOSCOW. With 8 full-page illustrations and a map.

The hero, Julian Wyatt, after several adventures with smugglers, by whom he is handed over a prisoner to the French, regains his freedom and joins Napoleon's army in the Russian campaign, and reaches Moscow with the victorious Emperor. Then, when the terrible retreat begins, Julian finds himself in the rear guard of the French army, fighting desperately, league by league, against famine, snow-storms, wolves, and Russians. Ultimately he escapes out of the general disaster, after rescuing the daughter of a Russian count; makes his way to St. Petersburg, and then returns to England. A story with an excellent plot, exciting adventures, and splendid historical interests.

G. A. HENTY'S POPULAR STORIES FOR BOYS

Each, crown 8vo, handsomely illustrated, $1.50.

IN THE HEART OF THE ROCKIES. A Story of Adventure in Colorado.

"One of the most interesting and attractive stories for boys. It is a tale of adventure thrilling enough for the most daring readers."—*Boston Journal*.

WULF THE SAXON. A Story of the Norman Conquest.

"An unusually realistic picture of the times. The scenes and incidents which Mr. Henty introduces are calculated to awaken fresh interest in the influence of the battle of Hastings upon the destiny of mankind."—*Boston Herald*.

WHEN LONDON BURNED. A Story of Restoration Times and the Great Fire.

"An exciting story of adventure, at the same time dealing with historic truths deftly and interestingly."—*Detroit Free Press*.

ST. BARTHOLOMEW'S EVE. A Tale of the Huguenot Wars.

"Exciting enough to interest even the dullest of readers."—*Boston Transcript*.

THROUGH THE SIKH WAR. A Tale of the Conquest of the Punjaub.

"Not only interesting but instructive. It is related with great spirit and animation."—*Boston Herald*.

A JACOBITE EXILE. Being the Adventures of a Young Englishman in the Service of Charles XII. of Sweden.

"Remarkable for its thrilling adventures and its interesting historical pictures."
—*Herald and Presbyter*.

BERIC THE BRITON. A Story of the Roman Invasion.

"It is a powerful and fascinating romance."—*Boston Post*.

IN GREEK WATERS. A Story of the Grecian War of Independence —1821-1827.

"It is a stirring narrative, wholesome and stimulating."—*Congregationalist*.

CONDEMNED AS A NIHILIST. A Story of Escape from Siberia.

"A narrative absorbing and thrilling. The scenes of Siberian prison-life give the book a peculiar value."—*Christian Advocate*.

REDSKIN AND COWBOY. A Tale of the Western Plains.

"Though it is full of hairbreadth escapes, none of the incidents are improbable. It is needless to say that the adventures are well told."—*San Francisco Chronicle*.

THE DASH FOR KHARTOUM. A Tale of the Nile Expedition.

HELD FAST FOR ENGLAND. A Tale of the Siege of Gibraltar.

The above are Mr. Henty's latest books. A full descriptive list containing all of Mr. Henty's books—now 47 in number—will be sent to any address on application. They are all attractively illustrated and handsomely bound.

SCRIBNER'S BOOKS FOR THE YOUNG

SAMUEL ADAMS DRAKE'S HISTORICAL BOOKS

THE MAKING OF THE OHIO VALLEY STATES. 1660-1837. Illustrated. 12mo, $1.50.

THE MAKING OF VIRGINIA AND THE MIDDLE COLONIES. 1578-7 Illustrated. 12mo, $1.50.

THE MAKING OF NEW ENGLAND. 1580-1643. With 148 illustrations and with maps. 12mo, $1.50.

THE MAKING OF THE GREAT WEST. 1812-1853. With 145 illustrations and with maps. 12mo, $1.50.

"The author's aim in these books is that they shall occupy a place between the larger and lesser histories of the lands and of the periods of which they treat, that each topic therein shall be treated as a unit and worked out to a clear understanding of its objects and results before passing to another topic. In the furtherance of this method each subject has its own descriptive notes, maps, plans, illustrations, the whole contributing to a thorough, though condensed, knowledge of the subject in hand."—*New York Mail and Express.*

POEMS OF CHILDHOOD BY EUGENE FIELD

LOVE SONGS OF CHILDHOOD. 16mo, $1.00.

WITH TRUMPET AND DRUM. By EUGENE FIELD. 16mo, $1.25.

"His poems of childhood have gone home, not only to the hearts of children, but to the heart of the country as well, and he is one of the few contributors to that genuine literature of childhood which expresses ideas from the stand-point of a child."—*The Outlook.*

THE NORSELAND SERIES

By H. H. BOYESEN.

NORSELAND TALES. Illustrated. 12mo, $1.25.

BOYHOOD IN NORWAY: NINE STORIES OF DEEDS OF THE SONS OF THE VIKINGS. With 8 illustrations. 12mo, $1.25.

AGAINST HEAVY ODDS, AND A FEARLESS TRIO. With 13 full-page illustrations by W. L. TAYLOR. 12mo, $1.25.

THE MODERN VIKINGS: STORIES OF LIFE AND SPORT IN THE NORSELAND. With many full-page illustrations. 12mo, $1.25.

The four above volumes in a box, $5.00.

"Charmingly told stories of boy-life in the Land of the Midnight Sun, illustrated with pictures giving a capital idea of the incidents and scenes described. The tales have a delight all their own, as they tell of scenes and sports and circumstances so different from those of our American life."—*New York Observer.*

TWO BOOKS BY ROSSITER JOHNSON

THE END OF A RAINBOW. AN AMERICAN STORY. Illustrated. 12mo, $1.50.

"It will be read with breathless interest. It is interesting and full of boyish experience."—*The Independent.*

PHAETON ROGERS. A NOVEL OF BOY LIFE. Illustrated. 12mo, $1.50.

MRS. BURTON HARRISON'S TALES

BRIC-A-BRAC STORIES. With 24 illustrations by WALTER CRANE. 12mo, $1.50.

"It is to be wished that every boy and girl might become acquainted with the contents of this book."—JULIAN HAWTHORNE.

THE OLD-FASHIONED FAIRY BOOK. Illustrated by ROSINA EMMET. 16mo, $1.25.

"The little ones, who so willingly go back with us to 'Jack the Giant Killer,' 'Bluebeard,' and the kindred stories of our childhood, will gladly welcome Mrs. Burton Harrison's 'Old-Fashioned Fairy Tales.'"—FRANK R. STOCKTON.

BOOKS OF ADVENTURE BY ROBERT LEIGHTON

OLAF THE GLORIOUS. A STORY OF OLAF TRIGGVISON, KING OF NORWAY, A.D. 995-1000. Crown 8vo, with numerous full-page illustrations, $1.50.

THE WRECK OF THE GOLDEN FLEECE. THE STORY OF A NORTH SEA FISHER BOY. Illustrated. Crown 8vo, $1.50.

THE THIRSTY SWORD. A STORY OF THE NORSE INVASION OF SCOTLAND, 1262-63. With 8 illustrations and a map. Crown 8vo, $1.50.

THE PILOTS OF POMONA. A STORY OF THE ORKNEY ISLANDS. With 8 illustrations and a map. Crown 8vo, $1.50.

"Mr. Leighton as a writer for boys needs no praise, as his books place him in the front rank."—*New York Observer.*

THINGS WILL TAKE A TURN

By BEATRICE HARRADEN, author of "Ships That Pass in the Night." Illustrated. 12mo, $1.00.

The charm of this tale is its delicate, wistful sympathy. It is the story of a sunny-hearted child, Rosebud, who assists her grandfather in his dusty, second-hand bookshop. One cannot help being fascinated by the sweet little heroine, she is so engaging, so natural; and to love Rosebud is to love all her friends and enter sympathetically into the good fortune she brought them.

AMONG THE LAWMAKERS

By EDMUND ALTON. Illustrated. Square 8vo, $1.50.

"The book is a diverting as well as an instructive one. Mr. Alton was in his early days a page in the Senate, and he relates the doings of Congress from the point of view he then obtained. His narrative is easy and piquant, and abounds in personal anecdotes about the great men whom the pages waited on."
—*Christian Union.*

EVENING TALES

DONE INTO ENGLISH FROM THE FRENCH OF FREDERIC ORTOLI, BY JOEL CHANDLER HARRIS. 12mo, $1.00.

"It is a veritable French 'Uncle Remus' that Mr. Harris has discovered in Frederic Ortoli. The book has the genuine piquancy of Gallic wit, and will be sure to charm American children. Mr. Harris's version is delightfully written."
—*Boston Beacon.*

HEROES OF THE OLDEN TIME

By JAMES BALDWIN. Three volumes, 12mo, each beautifully illustrated. Singly, $1.50; the set, $4.00.

A STORY OF THE GOLDEN AGE. Illustrated by HOWARD PYLE.

"Mr. Baldwin's book is redolent with the spirit of the Odyssey, that glorious primitive epic, fresh with the dew of the morning of time. It is an unalloyed pleasure to read his recital of the adventures of the wily Odysseus. Howard Pyle's illustrations render the spirit of the Homeric age with admirable felicity."
—Prof. H. H. BOYESEN.

THE STORY OF SIEGFRIED. Illustrated by HOWARD PYLE.

"The story of 'Siegfried' is charmingly told. The author makes up the story from the various myths in a fascinating way which cannot fail to interest the reader. It is as enjoyable as any fairy tale."—*Hartford Courant.*

THE STORY OF ROLAND. Illustrated by R. B. BIRCH.

"Mr. Baldwin has culled from a wide range of epics, French, Italian, and German, and has once more proved his aptitude as a story-teller for the young."
—*The Nation.*

THE BOY'S LIBRARY OF LEGEND AND CHIVALRY

Edited by SIDNEY LANIER, and richly illustrated by FREDERICKS, BENSELL, and KAPPES. Four volumes, cloth, uniform binding, price per set, $7.00. Sold separately, price per volume, $2.00.

Mr. Lanier's books present to boy readers the old English classics of history and legend in an attractive form. While they are stories of action and stirring incident, they teach those lessons which manly, honest boys ought to learn.

THE BOY'S KING ARTHUR

THE BOY'S FROISSART

THE BOY'S PERCY

THE KNIGHTLY LEGENDS OF WALES

FRANK R. STOCKTON'S BOOKS FOR THE YOUNG

"His books for boys and girls are classics."—*Newark Advertiser.*

THE CLOCKS OF RONDAINE, AND OTHER STORIES. With 24 illustrations by BLASHFIELD, ROGERS, BEARD, and others. Square 8vo, $1.50.

PERSONALLY CONDUCTED. Illustrated by PENNELL, PARSONS, and others. Square 8vo, $2.00.

THE STORY OF VITEAU. Illustrated by R. B. BIRCH. 12mo, $1.50.

A JOLLY FELLOWSHIP. With 20 illustrations. 12mo, $1.50.

THE FLOATING PRINCE AND OTHER FAIRY TALES. Illustrated. Square 8vo, $1.50.

THE TING-A-LING TALES. Illustrated. 12mo, $1.00.

ROUNDABOUT RAMBLES IN LANDS OF FACT AND FICTION. Illustrated. Square 8vo, $1.50.

TALES OUT OF SCHOOL. With nearly 200 illustrations. Square 8vo, $1.50.

"The volumes are profusely illustrated and contain the most entertaining sketches in Mr. Stockton's most entertaining manner."—*Christian Union.*

EDWARD EGGLESTON'S TWO POPULAR BOOKS

THE HOOSIER SCHOOL-BOY. Illustrated. 12mo, $1.00.

"'The Hoosier School-Boy' depicts some of the characteristics of boy-life years ago on the Ohio; characteristics, however, that were not peculiar to that section. The story presents a vivid and interesting picture of the difficulties which in those days beset the path of the youth aspiring for an education."
—*Chicago Inter-Ocean.*

QUEER STORIES FOR BOYS AND GIRLS. 12mo, $1.00.

"A very bright and attractive little volume for young readers. The stories are fresh, breezy, and healthy, with a good point to them and a good, sound American view of life and the road to success. The book abounds in good feeling and good sense, and is written in a style of homely art."—*Independent.*

HANS BRINKER

Or, THE SILVER SKATES. A Story of Life in Holland. By MARY MAPES DODGE. With 60 illustrations. 12mo, $1.50.

"The author has shown, in her former works for the young, a very rare ability to meet their wants; but she has produced nothing better than this charming tale—alive with incident and action, adorned rather than freighted with useful facts, and moral without moralization."—*The Nation.*

TWO BOOKS OF SPORTS AND GAMES

THE AMERICAN BOY'S HANDY BOOK; OR, WHAT TO DO AND HOW TO DO IT. By DANIEL C. BEARD. With 360 illustrations by the author. Square 8vo, $2.00.

"The book has this great advantage over its predecessors, that most of the games, tricks, and other amusements described in it are new. It treats of sports adapted to all seasons of the year; it is practical, and it is well illustrated."
—*New York Tribune.*

THE AMERICAN GIRL'S HANDY BOOK. By LENA and ADELIA B. BEARD. With over 500 illustrations by the authors. Square 8vo, $2.00.

"I have put it in my list of good and useful books for young people, as I have many requests for advice from my little friends and their anxious mothers. I am most happy to commend your very ingenious and entertaining book."
LOUISA M. ALCOTT.

THOMAS NELSON PAGE'S TWO BOOKS

AMONG THE CAMPS; OR, YOUNG PEOPLE'S STORIES OF THE WAR. With 8 full-page illustrations. Square 8vo, $1.50.

"They are five in number, each having reference to some incident of the Civil War. A vein of mingled pathos and humor runs through them all, and greatly heightens the charm of them. It is the early experience of the author himself, doubtless, which makes his pictures of life in a Southern home during the great struggle so vivid and truthful."—*The Nation.*

TWO LITTLE CONFEDERATES. With 8 full-page illustrations by KEMBLE and REDWOOD. Square 8vo, $1.50.

"Mr. Page was 'raised' in Virginia, and he knows the 'darkey' of the South better than any one who writes about them. And he knows 'white folks,' too and his stories, whether for old or young people, have the charm of sincerity and beauty and reality."—*Harper's Young People.*

www.ingramcontent.com/pod-product-compliance
Lightning Source LLC
Chambersburg PA
CBHW021817230426
43669CB00008B/783